AF646990

Black Money in India

Meaning, Magnitude and Measures

Chitra Lele

ATLANTIC
PUBLISHERS & DISTRIBUTORS (P) LTD

Published by
ATLANTIC
PUBLISHERS & DISTRIBUTORS (P) LTD
7/22, Ansari Road, Darya Ganj, New Delhi-110002
Phones : +91-11-40775252, 23273880, 23275880, 23280451
Fax : +91-11-23285873
Web : www.atlanticbooks.com
E-mail : orders@atlanticbooks.com

Branch Office
5, Nallathambi Street, Wallajah Road, Chennai-600002
Phones : +91-44-64611085, 32413319
E-mail : chennai@atlanticbooks.com

Copyright © Chitra Lele, 2018

All rights reserved. No part of this publication may be reproduced, stored in a retrieval system, transmitted or utilized in any form or by any means, electronic, mechanical, photocopying, recording or otherwise, without the prior permission of the copyright owner. Application for such permission should be addressed to the publisher.

Disclaimer

The author and the publisher have taken every effort to the maximum of their skill, expertise and knowledge to provide correct material in the book. Even then if some mistakes persist in the content of the book, the publisher does not take responsibility for the same. The publisher shall have no liability to any person or entity with respect to any loss or damage caused, or alleged to have been caused directly or indirectly, by the information contained in this book.

The publisher has fully tried to follow the copyright law. However, if any work is found to be similar, it is unintentional and the same should not be used as defamatory or to file legal suit against the author/publisher.

If the readers find any mistakes, we shall be grateful to them for pointing out those to us so that they can be corrected in the next edition.

All disputes are subject to the jurisdiction of Delhi court only.

Printed in India at Nice Printing Press, A-33/3A, Site-IV, Industrial Area, Sahibabad, Ghaziabad, U.P.

Foreword

Even though Chitra Lele has come into my literary friendship for just two years now, she has conquered my mind with her amazing literary talents which are seldom found among young writers of the world. Her world record performances in the field of peace making and literature astonish the young and the old alike. It seems that there are very few cliffs of literary fame before her to conquer. Thus, when she approached me for a foreword I couldn't say 'no' even though I have been very busy with my editorial activities. Rather I took it as an honor to read this book titled *Black Money in India: Meaning, Magnitude and Measures* and write a fitting foreword for it.

More people today are ready to fight the menace of black money in India than ever before, and yet, very few know what it takes to achieve this aim as the dynamics of black money are complex and deep. The young and sensitive author, Chitra Lele, attempts to break down these dynamics into clear, simple and emphatic aspects of *who, when, where, why, how, what,* and *what next* of black money, with a hope of triggering intellectual discussions and a doable agenda against this cancer.

The author exposes how the intricate web of corrupt elements (politicians, bureaucrats, corporations, judges, lobbyists, etc.) has engulfed the economy, social order, national exchequer and moral foundation of India through its spurious practices and abuse of power. The book deals with the causes, effects and methods of black money in detail. The book discusses the detrimental effects of various black money channels like money laundering, political funding, hawala transactions, terrorism funding, round tripping, etc., and these effects are demonstrated through eye-opening statistics and data.

Chitra not only focuses on the basic and advanced dynamics of black money in India, but also discusses at length the global black money scenarios and statistics to present to the readers a holistic picture of this peril gnawing at the very foundation on which our world stands. The book throws light on various past anti-black money measures like voluntary disclosure schemes, demonetization, etc., and their pros and cons, and at the same time, presents a revised and comprehensive multi-pronged strategy as to how to minimize black money. She gives a blueprint of how the key stakeholders of India and the world, including the government setup, business world, media, human rights groups, civil society, and international development agencies can help to curb black money transactions and flows occurring at the national and international interfaces.

This book is Chitra's earnest attempt to help everyone, right from policymakers to civil society members, and from scholars to *aam aadmi* (common man), to comprehend the breadth and depth of the magnitude of black money. Never before has the call for good governance been greater. Never before has the call for social collective action been louder. I am sure this book will broaden and deepen the voice of the people in bringing the black money players to book, and in ensuring equal opportunities of growth to one and all. That is why you should read on....

Prof. Dr. K.V. Dominic
Retired Associate Professor of English,
Newman College, Thodupuzha, Kerala,
Author, Critic, Editor and Publisher

Preface

Black money is the root cause of all the evils in the world. Concentration of wealth and power in the wrong hands breed black money. Black money breeds black money. The fuel for running the wheels of black money is black money. In the post-independence period, India has lost a whopping 500+ billion US dollars through black money, black money and illicit financial flows. When India's black money is equal to around a fifth of its Gross Domestic Product, it is high time that we as vigilant citizens of the country put pressure on the Indian Government and the tax havens to release information on the black money accounts, and the money in these accounts should be brought back to the country and then used to solve many economic and social problems.

Most people have a nebulous notion of black money; hence they have limited knowledge about it and are not able to come together to fight against this menace. This is where my book *Black Money in India: Meaning, Magnitude and Measures* steps in to fill these gaps in knowledge. This book will take the readers beyond the myopic view. The main motivation for writing this book is to bring out the dynamics of black money in India in the public domain so that each and every one understands how entrenched this cancer is in India. Through my book, I want to spark up more and more discussions and debates in the academic communities, public forums and common man *kattas* (kattas are platforms or benches built around trees where commoners gather to discuss matters, both mundane and serious). It is sad to witness how tax laws and the incentives for promoting charitable causes are misused in the garb of non-profit motives. It is such a shame!

The corrupt political leadership, the scandalous corporate elites and the dishonest bureaucrats are all partners in crime in this dirty game of black money. A politician hoards loads of black money through vote bank politics. A businessman uses black money to influence political policies. A bureaucrat possesses piles of black money through bribes and kickbacks. The book discusses the basic as well as advanced dynamics of this parallel money behind all the mayhem. As it is evident from various studies, articles and statistics, black money in the hands of criminals has been parked in offshore bank accounts, high-rise apartments, posh cars, exorbitant vacations, etc. They enjoy all the facilities and luxuries at our cost—we pay for their lavish lifestyle with our hard-earned money—to the last penny.

The book is divided into three main sections through which it covers the A to Z of black money:

1. Apart from dealing with fundamental topics like the definition, history, characteristics and causes, the book also provides comprehensive information about the role of politics in the generation of black money.
2. The other major players of black money like the corporate world, bureaucracy, etc., are dealt with in detail.
3. The book also elucidates the effects of black money on the Indian economy, national exchequer and society.
4. The magnitude and the reach of black money in India along with statistics are discussed.
5. The global black money scenarios along with statistics are shared.
6. The various past anti-black money measures and policies along with proposed future measures and policies are discussed.
7. All of that and much more.

All the features and tools needed to facilitate quick understanding of the phenomenon of black money are included in the book: tables that provide eye-opening statistics, examples that clarify concepts, spotlight and a word of caution sections to highlight important points, chapter recap, and questions for reflection.

This book has been written for every Indian and global citizen, right from policymakers to civil society members, and from scholars to *aam aadmi* (common man). It is a genuine attempt to build a collective momentum and public support for matters of national and global significance, especially for tackling the global crisis of black money.

Chitra Lele

Acknowledgements

This book, while an individual work, benefited from the insights and direction of several people. I use this opportunity to express my heartfelt thanks to all those who supported me in one way or the other during the completion of this writing project.

What I have learned over the years comes as a result of being a daughter of wonderful parents—Mrs. Asha Lele and Mr. G.G. Lele. They have been the motivation that has helped me to maintain laser-sharp focus on my goals. Thanks to them for their ongoing support and endless encouragement.

I offer my deep gratitude to the Divine Essence for bestowing on me the strength to follow my heart.

I owe my deepest gratitude to Dr. K.V. Dominic for writing the scholarly Foreword for my book. I tender my heartfelt gratitude to Dominic Sir for evincing keen interest in my book.

While developing the manuscript, my discussions and debates with experts from various fields was highly value adding.

I owe my sincere gratitude to my company colleagues who gave me the time and space to complete this book. Their ceaseless cooperation in adjusting to my project work schedule and writing schedule helped me to maintain balance between these two aspects.

I am extremely grateful to the Atlantic Publishers Team for their constructive comments and persistent support. Their editorial feedback, design inputs and constant reviews have transformed this writing project into an informative and interesting book.

A very special 'thank you' must go to you all, my readers, for investing your time in reading my book.

Last but not least, I beg forgiveness of all those who have been with me over the course of the years and whose names I have failed to mention. Your support and encouragement is deeply appreciated by me.

Without the support of all those mentioned, this book would have been far more difficult and the results less satisfying.

Chitra Lele

Contents

Part 3
Measures for Curbing Black Money in India

List of Tables

PART 1
Introduction, Meaning, Causes and Much More

Chapter 1

The Basics of Black Money in India

Black money (also called parallel economy or underground economy) has been a serious subject of concern for India since the past many years. It is a major hindrance in achieving good governance and in allowing India to realize her full potential. Although black money in India is a decades-old phenomenon, it has become a real threat since the post-liberalization period. Tax is a critical source for reallocation of resources, but by evading taxes the entire nation is found in a crippling position. As black money is the money that is unaccounted for; hence giving an accurate estimate for it is not possible. There are many estimates of the amount of black money stashed abroad. The Global Financial Integrity (GFI is US-based think tank on international finances that works to curtail illicit financial flows) puts the number at 440 billion dollars. The Central Bureau of Investigation (CBI is the premier investigating agency in India) puts the black money estimate at 500 billion dollars. Yet another research statistic estimate pegs the black money economy at 62 percent of the Gross Domestic Product (GDP is the value of a country's overall output of goods and services that helps in gauging the health of the country's economy), i.e., 1.4 trillion dollars. In 2010, the World Bank shared the estimates of the size of black money in India between 1999 and 2007; the Table 1 is given as follows.

Table 1: Year-wise Size of Black Money in India between 1999 and 2007

Year	Black Money as a Percent of Gross Domestic Product
1999	23.2
2000	23.1
2001	22.8
2002	22.6
2003	22.3
2004	22.0
2005	21.7
2006	21.2
2007	20.7

Table Source: World Bank Estimates

It is no secret that black money has been flowing out of India into Swiss banks and other tax havens. India contributes 10 percent of the billions (21 billion dollars) illegally moved out of developing and emerging nations (this estimate is from the research report 2014 by Global Financial Integrity). This goes to show that the volume and complexity of black money stemming from the parallel economy of India is growing at an alarming rate. The parallel economy has social, moral, economic, legal, ethical, and political implications. The circulation of black money is referred to as "parallel economy" or "underground economy" or "shadow economy".

The depth and the spread of black money have often been extensively discussed and debated through various platforms and for me I am using this book as a tool to trigger actionable intelligence and balanced discussions in order to come up with doable solutions to curb or minimize this menace.

A recent survey by Transparency International (TI is an anti-corruption global civil society organization leading the fight against corruption) states that India has the highest bribery rate among the 16 Asia Pacific countries surveyed. Another glaring statistic showed that India has the highest bribery rate of all the nations surveyed for access to basic public services. According to 2016 results of the Corruption Perception Index of Transparency International, India ranks at the 79th place out of 176 nations.

Many economists and researchers have stated that cash as a black money component is just one player of this parallel economy game, the other components include foreign exchange, jewelry, gold and property.

> **Spotlight**
>
> A report by Global Financial Integrity (GFI) stated that the total illicit outflows from India were pegged at 165 billion dollars between 2005 and 2014 and illicit inflows in India between 2005 and 2014 were pegged at 770 billion dollars.

1.1 DEFINITION OF BLACK MONEY

Black money is tax-evaded income. There is no standard, universally accepted definition of black money in academic literature or academic communities. Even under the Black Money (Undisclosed Foreign Income and Assets) and Imposition of Tax Act, 2015, black money does not have any formal definition. The Wanchoo Committee Report (Government of India, Ministry of Finance, 1971) depicted the black money phenomenon as a "cancerous growth in the country's economy which, if not checked in time, will surely lead to its ruination". Another widely used definition is found in the 1985 report on Aspects of Black Economy by the National Institute of Public Finance and Policy (NIPFP is a leading centre for research in public economics and policies) which defined black income as "the aggregates of incomes which are taxable but not reported to the tax authorities".

As per the White Paper issued on Black Money by the Government of India in May 2012, "Black money is defined as assets or resources that have neither been reported to the public authorities at the time of their generation nor disclosed at any point of time during their possession."

There is no fixed academic definition. In common language, black money refers to income illegally obtained or not declared for tax purposes. It is usually received in cash from the activities carried out in the parallel economy. In common parlance, black money refers to the unsanctioned sector in the economy whose operations and objectives run parallel but in contradiction with the operations and objectives of the legitimate economy. Black money is not merely about counterfeit or fake money; it is much more than that.

Sources of black money include transactions involving stolen goods, terrorism, selling pirated material, terrorism activity, drug trafficking, etc. The players of this black game must spend the money in the black economy, or must stash it away in secret places like tax havens, or must use methods like money laundering to conceal their income source. Money laundering is the process of making illegally-gained proceeds appear as legal; it is used to conceal the source, identity and destination of such illegal proceeds. It can be earned both through illegal and legal means. In the legal means, the income earned by people is not fully disclosed for tax purpose (avoidance), for example, teachers earning over and above their official salary through tuitions, government doctors who earn extra money through their private practice, and there are many more such instances.

Another definition is given by the *Collins Dictionary* (a printed and online dictionary of English published by HarperCollins), "that part of a nation's income that relates to its black economy and any money that a person or organization acquires illegally, as by a means that involves tax evasion".

Some experts include unaccounted money or concealed income and/or undisclosed wealth while defining black money, while some others imply that only clandestine transactions are related to black money, and many experts consider these explanations as a narrow view of black money. For the third category of experts, black money denotes not only unaccounted money which is either hoarded or is in circulation outside the official economy, but also its investment in precious stones, land, properties, gold, etc.

Spotlight

From the definitions, we can conclude that the concept of black money has two connotations attached to it—it is money earned by violating laws, legal norms, moral norms and social norms, and such money is usually undisclosed and kept secret. We can add yet another connotation—money which is not included in national income estimates.

Of late, another dimension to black money has been added by a faction who runs digital and credit card business setups and this dimension is that of including all money which is not digitally transacted. Hence the definition of black money keeps gaining more and more layers of meaning. But this does not mean that the sincere people who transact only in cash are criminals. There are millions of honest citizens who have stayed away from the tax net because they are either daily wage earners who subsist on a day-to-day basis or are allowed to stay outside the tax net by convention or law.

1.2 CHARACTERISTICS OF BLACK MONEY

1. **Earned through Illegal Means**—the proceeds are earned from illegal sources and transactions. There are several sources of black money which are used for earning and further circulating it in the shadow economy: tax havens, interest earned from unorganized credit markets, public procurement, black marketing, unauthorized sale of licenses and permits, illegal gratification in the form of *pagdi* or *salami* (it is a one-time, hefty down payment made by a tenant to a landlord, and the transaction of payment and receipt is done in unaccounted cash to avoid paying taxes and to circumvent rent control legislation), unaccounted stock market profit, etc. All these activities are punishable under the legal framework of a nation.

2. **Tax Evasion and Avoidance**—people intentionally avoid paying their tax dues, custom duties, etc., and evade taxes, price controls and administrative procedures—they are involved in under-reporting or non-reporting of income. Another group is people who fail to declare their tax returns to the tax authorities by virtue of ignorance. In the case of ignorance, the transactions

and activities undertaken by the person/s could be legitimate and otherwise permissible under the law of the land but s/he has failed to report the income to the appropriate authority.

3. Social Impact—black money affects the economy and erodes it completely. It has an even bigger implication: social impact. The problem of unemployment affects the unemployed section of society and poverty affects the poor, but black money does not really affect the ones who possess it, rather it adversely affects the common man.

In India, 90 percent of the resources are in the hands of 1 percent, the common man represents the remaining 99 percent. And this common man has to bear the brunt of all ill-effects caused by black money.

4. Legitimate Means—apart from the illegal sources of earning black money, there are several white-collared, legitimate means also available where money is earned through legal means but not declared for tax evasion purpose. For example, teachers earning money through private tuitions, unbanked savings, etc.

5. Cash Dealings—cash dealings or cash usage is the prime method of carrying out black money deals and transactions as it does not leave any evidence, transaction trail or footprint or paper trail.

6. Clandestine Channels—black money involves the transfer of money and funds from India to foreign nations through clandestine channels. Highly controlled products and substances like firearms and drugs are mainly traded/smuggled through the clandestine channels of the black market. Black money deals usually take place "under the table". Black money generated from clandestine channels is often used to operate terror networks.

1.3 HISTORY OF BLACK MONEY IN INDIA

Tax is a significant resource of revenue mobilization that can be used for the betterment of a nation. Unfortunately the world history and the Indian history show that black money and tax evasion have always been the forerunner across all sectors and sections of the society.

1.3.1 Pre-Independence History

In India, income tax levy was introduced for the first time in 1860 by James Wilson, the first finance member in Viceroy Lord Canning's council. The tax evasion and accumulation of black money began during the Second World War leading to the tax evaded incomes finding their stash spots in the Swiss Bank accounts. Moreover, the rapid growth of international trade following the Second World War created more opportunities for the international movement of capital, which resulted in a more complex international taxation system; hence more opportunities to evade taxes and generate unaccounted income.

Terms like black market and black money became popular during the war and in the post-war period. The history of black money in India in the pre-Independence period can be traced back to the 1940s, when the rationing system was introduced as part of the food security system through the public distribution system in the form of a network of ration shops also known as fair price shops. In the past, controls over price and distribution have resulted in the generation of black money on a huge scale. Price controls in the absence of an adequate system of distribution and an ineffective arrangement for increasing supplies had resulted in huge amounts black money being generated in the past. The licensing system required a large number of inspectors to execute various functions and formalities, which meant that an equally large amount of money had to be paid 'under-the-table'. And where controls could not be implemented, one saw a lot of harassment and black money generation.

The Second World War set the stage for widespread corruption in modern times. The supply of industrial goods to the Allies was cut off during the war from their suppliers due to transport problems, and this led to a severe shortage of vital goods. The British used this aspect to their advantage by implementing inflationary tactics which led to sharp rise in prices. This rise led to huge profits and prompted many to indulge in tax evasion. This also encouraged businessmen to sell goods which were supply deficient in the black market for excessive profits. The mafia also took control of the sectors where there was shortage, generating huge amounts of black money. This tendency gave rise to the psychology that more money can be earned through evading taxes rather than doing business with fair means and earning legally. Unfortunately, this psychology is rampant in today's times as well.

In the Indian context, taxes and their meaning can be traced back to Chanakya's (Chanakya was an Indian teacher, economist, philosopher and royal advisor) celebrated treatise and magnum opus, 'Arthashastra'; Arthashastra is a Sanskrit term which is translated as "The Science of Material Gain". It covers the different types of taxes and the punishments for evading them. Chanakya has detailed out the several ways of embezzling funds by government officials that led to the generation of black money even in those times of 4th century BC. In his treatise, he had listed at least 40 ways of doing so, right from *avastara* (fabrication of accounts) to *pratibandha* (obstruction). Chanakya advocated stringent oversight and control of all economic activities in order to safeguard and support sources of income for the state and its inhabitants. Incomes were classified as coming from various parts of the kingdom and from various sectors (private and state run). Chanakya had installed an extensive system of spies to keep an eye on the entire official machinery and another system of spies to keep an eye on the spies themselves. The state had many *Adhyakshas* (heads) who were responsible for different departments and their incomes from taxes. A separate *Akshatpataladhyaksh* (Comptroller and Auditor General) was also set up for preparing and auditing state accounts. Chanakya had set up departments with *adhyakshas* or heads, and officials to assist them to ensure that all incomes and expenditures of their respective departments were accurately estimated and the correct taxes were levied, and there were penalties for levying both too little and too much taxes. But this oversight and control factor has always been missing in the Indian state of affairs since the beginning of modern times.

The age old method practiced in India of "kacha bill" and "pakka bill" is yet another source of age old black money. A "kacha bill" is a bill/invoice on which a consumer need not pay any tax on the value of the good purchased from the seller of goods, and this in turn make the sellers buy goods from distributors/wholesalers in the same fashion. Therefore this chain reaction results in a never-ending cycle of tax evasion. Dealings done in this manner are not accounted for in the account books of the traders and sellers. As there is no paying of income tax on the income from the transaction of sales and purchases, direct tax is evaded or avoided. As there no liability for paying sales tax, excise duty, etc., indirect tax is evaded or avoided. This age old practice is very much alive even in modern times.

Spotlight

Arthashastra had shlokas (a shloka is a Sanskrit verse) related to minting of coins. The treatise discussed various provisions related to certifying the authenticity of coins by a coin examiner, punishment to counterfeiters, collection of charges and taxes on coins, etc. Black money and fake currency were major issues back then also.

The political and administrative corruption and the entrenched black economy in India have been there right from day one of the annals of Indian history.

1.3.2 Recent History of Black Money

When the British took over India and its operations, the British realized that the vast discretionary powers given to their administrators would lead to embezzlement of funds from the national coffers. In order to minimize this possibility, the British ensured that the British officers posted in India would be given high salaries. When India gained independence, the same colonial administration setup was maintained by the Indian Government, but the salaries of the administrators were reduced drastically. This drastic cut made the poorly paid public employees indulge in practices of earning illegal incomes to compensate for their low salaries. They misused their vast discretionary powers. And these practices have spread fast and deep, and far and wide across all levels of the Indian administrative setup.

The Indian condition worsened with the introduction of a tax scheme designed in such a way that by the 1970s, the highest earners were required to pay about 93.5 percent in tax. And, in some cases, the combined taxes in various categories exceeded the actual income. In many cases, it was simply not possible to survive if one paid these taxes. This irrational tax regime led to tax evasion which resulted in corruption and black money on a massive scale.

In its first party document, released on October 21, 1951, the Jana Sangh (it was a nationalist political party that existed from 1951 to 1977) referred to a "horde of problems" besetting India, both "internal and external, old and new, which instead of nearing solution after independence are daily getting aggravated.... Its production is falling, black marketing and profiteering are rampant and charges of corruption and favoritism against the administration are growing." Jana Sangh's economic resolution, 'Economic Situation in the Throes of a Holocaust', in its 1974 session, stated clearly on the need to eradicate black money: "The Indian economy is diseased, and present order of privileges, licenses, black money, and quotas is suffering from incurable cancer."

There was widespread black money and corruption at the top, middle and bottom tiers of governance in the Indian subcontinent during the import substitution industrialization regime (ISI is a trade and economic policy that aims to decrease dependence on developed nations by replacing foreign imports with domestic production). India adopted the import substitution industrialization during the fifties. Economic reforms during this period became a source of huge one-time rents to politicians in power, for example, privatization of public monopolies. This reduced their ability to use the public sector for political patronage in the future. Hence as time went by, they found newer ways to mint money by looting the national exchequer, non-disclosure of political funding, lobbying, etc.

Independent India started off on the wrong footing with a weak democratic model. The power and control was transferred from the colonial rulers to their Indian political counterparts without much change in the ground rules and administrative norms. The Indian politicians were still under the influence of the power elite and this set the stage for corruption and black money at an even higher level. The big business houses used their clout to influence political policy and agenda by directly exerting their control over political parties by providing funds for the electoral campaigns. They used their influence to also affect the bureaucratic appointments.

In the period after 1991—post-liberation—politicians and businesses started to mingle openly. Even though tax rates and controls had been drastically relaxed by then, the black economy still continued to expand. Many politicians became businessmen and vice versa. The triad of politicians, businessmen and bureaucrats found new opportunities for making black money through deals and transactions related to sectors like mines, lands, etc. Today, this triad has grown so strong that these players get away with their crimes and the common man has to face the music caused by the chaos created by these miscreants, always.

In India, direct taxation on income and wealth was very high till recent years, which made people find ways of evading taxes. Until a decade ago, the marginal income tax rate was as high as 75 percent. Similarly, corporate tax rates were considerably high that made corporations evade taxes.

During the Second World War, India experienced a serious shortage in essential items and the Indian Government resorted to a system of controls and rationing of these items. Instead of food security, food theft had become the name of the game where commoners were deprived from having basic food items caused by artificial scarcity and inflationary prices. The License Raj also added to the black money and corruption levels. Although the then Indian Government introduced the licensing system and controls to make India a planned economy where the state would control all aspects of the economy, but in reality, the political power was misused to amass unaccounted wealth in return for favors granted to the business world. The License Raj has since been replaced by a policy of economic liberalization, but the after-effects of the evils of black money it brought on into the society still exist to this very day. As a result, black money has been a part of the Indian society, both during the pre-reform and post-reform periods.

In recent times, the demonetization of 500 and 1000 rupee notes November 2016 has unleashed a furious debate in India on taxation, corruption, the informal cash economy, counterfeiting of notes and so on. As with the previous demonetization drives, this drive too caused hardships to innocent people like the common man, small businesses, village folk, daily wage earners, homemakers and honest taxpayers. There are different theoretical views on the pros and cons of this measure, which we will discuss later on in the book. As a result of the past and recent history of black money, the Indian landscape is steeped in endemic corruption and black money.

A Word of Caution

Whether it is the past history of black money or the recent history of black money, one cannot expect to curtail it by going soft on the three main pillars of the nation (the legislature, the executive, and the judiciary). Most of the anti-black money measures till date have always targeted the wrong people, i.e., honest taxpayers and law-abiding citizens. The layers of black money from the three main pillars need to be weeded out first, only then the other layers (corporate, press, etc.) can be peeled away.

1.4 CAUSES OF BLACK MONEY

Black money is generated through a plethora of transactions and activities like misuse of public property, payment of bribes, manipulation of expenses, misappropriation of public funds, evasion of taxes, etc.

1. Corruption and Crime—is the major cause of generating black money. The 'corrupt' component of black money includes bribes, policy changes and business grants for financial favors. The 'criminal' component of black money includes activities like extortion, forgery, ammunition and explosives, smuggling of goods, contraband goods, human trafficking, financial fraud, illegal mining, embezzlement, etc.

2. Ineffective Enforcement of Tax Laws—research has shown that nations with poor or ineffective implementation of tax laws and regulations tend to have a higher share of the unaccounted economy. While India is good at making laws, it is equally ineffective in implementing the same. The new black money law has been criticized heavily as it is meant to prosecute and punish Indians with illegal foreign incomes and assets, while the much bigger problem of black money is the domestic economy which has not been addressed at all. Again most experts and critics believe that this new law too will not make much of a difference, as India already has in place several laws dealing with tax evasion and money laundering like the Foreign Exchange and Management Act, 1999, the Income Tax Act, 1961, etc., which are poorly enforced. This new law has been criticized on yet another account: too much discretion being granted to tax officials could be misused and this in turn could dampen India's investment climate, deter even people who want to open up a legitimate foreign account, etc.

3. **Faulty Social Practices and Norms**—in the Indian society and culture, the practices of tax evasion and black money are not seen as a taboo; they are quite acceptable. And the practice of paying one's tax dues sincerely is not seen as a virtue either.

4. **Quota System**—quota system introduced in all sectors is misused to generate black money. The Indian Government has a fixed quota for import, export and foreign exchange, and this quota system is misused to make more black money. Right from education to employment, the quota system opens the doors to the world of black market.

5. **Bribes**—bribes in India are considered a necessary evil. Right from the public to sole proprietors and from medium enterprises to big corporations, everyone greases somebody's palms to get their work done faster. Black money is often associated with illegal activities such as bribes.

Measures, including demonetization, do not really deter corrupt officials, both blue collar and white collar, from taking graft, in some other form (like gold).

6. **Faulty Taxation and Laws**—faulty tax laws and structure lead to black money. High tax rates deter people from declaring their income and make them indulge in ways that help them in

evading taxes. In spite of the fact that there a number of laws related to various taxes, they still do not deter black money hoarders as these various tax-related departments themselves are deeply entrenched in corruption. Due to high tax rates, tax evasion is common in corporate tax, income tax, sales tax, custom duties, etc.

Usually, high tax rates, either perceived or actual, provide a strong motivation to evade taxes and generate black money. High tax rates increase the tendency of not to pay taxes and not to comply with the tax laws of the country, and this is achieved by resorting to black money inflows exchanged between the givers and takers. A report submitted by the National Institute of Public Finance and Policy (NIPFP) to the finance ministry estimated that black money would exceed 10 percent or more of GDP; this study was commissioned by NIPFP in the last week of December 2012 in order to quantify the black money that was generated in India. This estimate shows that the black money generated is much more than the central budget of the Indian Government.

Although the Indian tax system has a wide range of regulations and laws for sales tax, income tax, stamp duty and excise duty, extensive corruption in all the departments has rendered their enforcement ineffective.

7. **Manipulations of Accounts**—there are several ways of manipulating accounts books. Some tax evaders maintain parallel books of accounts wherein in order to evade reporting of transactions or the income from them, the tax evaders maintain two accounts books: one for tax authorities like income tax, sales tax, etc., and one for their own consumption with the aim of managing their business setup. The first one is manipulated in several ways like inflating expenses, omitting receipts, etc. Another way of evading taxes and generating black income is through 'out of book' transactions wherein the tax evaders either do not maintain any accounts books or maintain two sets or record only certain transactions.

Other types of manipulation tactics include manipulation of expenses (labor charges, raw material expenses, etc.) through obtaining inflated or bogus invoices and vouchers. Serious manipulation of expenses includes "hawala" transactions. Hawala means a parallel remittance system and it operates in parallel to traditional financial channels and banking system. In hawala transactions, transfer of money occurs based on the communication and trust among a network of hawala dealers. It is a common practice to use partial names or codes for hawala brokers.

8. **Illegal Valuables and Holdings**—one of the most popular methods of stashing away black money is in the form of precious gems and metals. The Indian media is rife with reports of raids carried out in the businessmen and celebrity homes where holdings and valuables worth crores are seized.

9. **Scarcity of Resources**—is a major cause for black money. Scarcity of resources, either real or artificial, and a faulty public distribution system generate black money. Shortage of essential goods causes people to pay higher than the market-controlled price, and this results in illegal black money transactions.

10. **Transfer Activities**—giving and taking bribes in India is rampant. Such transfer activities lead to the creation of the culture of easy money. This culture corrupts the social fabric and also discourages honest taxpayers and entrepreneurs.

11. **Transactions through Associate Enterprises**—fraudulent persons and organizations make use of transactions through associate enterprise that operate through various geographic locations taking (dis)advantage of various tax regimes.

12. **Inflation**—it is both the cause as well as the consequence of the unstoppable growth of black money in India. The increasing prices of resources like oil, petrol, etc., in the international markets, jag up the prices of these commodities when they reach the Indian shores due to the high taxes and duties imposed by the government, and this causes inflation and in turn leads to the generation of black money.

13. **Real Estate Transactions**—there is a growing trend towards converting agriculture/agrarian land into asset-based property; this proposition is considered highly profitable. Real estate dealers, agents and customers pounce on such

opportunities. With the large gap between market values and registration values, there is a huge scope for black money transactions. The strong presence of black money in the real estate section has resulted into skyrocketed prices. According to one study, it will take an Indian with the average per capita income 580 years to buy a top-end property in Mumbai, compared to 65 years in Hong Kong, 62 years in Paris, and 47 years in New York. Builders indulge in black money practices in order to save time and avoid all the bureaucratic hurdles.

Officials give builders land plots at throw-away prices and then manipulate land-use rules to pump up the value of these plots. These rising land prices also fuel inflation; inflation again is a major source of black money. Under-reporting of transaction price, real estate deals in the form of capital gains tax and stamp duty can lead to tax evasion.

> **Spotlight**
>
> It is high time that the Indian Government stops this real estate menace and ensures that all players in this game view land not as money-making machine but as a limited resource that needs to be used for the public good.

14. Electoral Funding—according to the Centre for Media Studies (CMS is a market research company and an academic resource center), approximately 4.9 billion dollars were spent during the latest election campaigns of 2014. This means that these elections were the second-most expensive elections after the 2012 US election campaign that cost 6 billion dollars. Today contesting elections has become a very costly affair.

15. Under-invoiced Inventories—people use this method in which the amount of inventory is under-invoiced so that they can use the excess amount to sale in the black market. Such transactions are never reported officially and are not accounted for in the accounts books.

1.5 CHAPTER RECAP

1. Although black money in India is a decades-old phenomenon, it has become a real threat since the post-

liberalization period. Tax is a critical source for reallocation of resources, but by evading taxes the entire nation is found in a crippling position.

2. It is no secret that black money has been flowing out of India into Swiss banks and other tax havens. India contributes 10 percent of the billions (21 billion dollars) illegally moved out of developing and emerging nations (this estimate is from the research report 2014 by Global Financial Integrity (GFI is a Washington-based think tank on international finances).

3. A recent survey by Transparency International (TI is an anti-corruption global civil society organization leading the fight against corruption) states that India has the highest bribery rate among the 16 Asia Pacific countries surveyed. According to 2016 results of the Corruption Perception Index of Transparency International, India ranks at the 79th place out of 176 nations.

4. Black money is tax-evaded income. There is no standard, universally accepted definition of black money in academic literature or academic communities. Even under the Black Money (Undisclosed Foreign Income and Assets) and Imposition of Tax Act, 2015, black money does not have any formal definition. The Wanchoo Committee Report (Government of India, Ministry of Finance, 1971) depicted the black money phenomenon as a "cancerous growth in the country's economy which, if not checked in time, will surely lead to its ruination". Another widely used definition is found in the 1985 report on Aspects of Black Economy by the National Institute of Public Finance and Policy (NIPFP is a leading centre for research in public economics and policies) which defined black income as "the aggregates of incomes which are taxable but not reported to the tax authorities".

5. Sources of black money include transactions involving stolen goods, terrorism, selling pirated material, terrorism activity, drug trafficking, etc. The players of this black game must spend the money in the black economy, or must stash it away in secret places like tax havens, or must use methods like money laundering to conceal their income source.

6. Many economists and researchers have stated that cash as a black money component is just one player of this parallel economy game, the other components include foreign exchange, jewelry, gold and property.

7. Tax is a significant resource of revenue mobilization that can be used for the betterment of a nation. Unfortunately the world history and the Indian history show that black money and tax evasion have always been the forerunner across all sectors and sections of the society.

8. The tax evasion and accumulation of black money began during the Second World War leading to the tax evaded incomes finding their stash spots in the Swiss Bank accounts. Moreover, the rapid growth of international trade following the Second World War created more opportunities for the international movement of capital, which resulted in a more complex international taxation system; hence more opportunities to evade taxes and generate unaccounted income.

9. In the Indian context, taxes and their meaning can be traced back to Chanakya's (Chanakya was an Indian teacher, economist, philosopher and royal advisor) celebrated treatise and magnum opus, 'Arthashastra'; Arthashastra is a Sanskrit term which is translated as "The Science of Material Gain". It covers the different types of taxes and the punishments for evading them.

10. Independent India started off on the wrong footing with a weak democratic model. The power and control was transferred from the colonial rulers to their Indian political counterparts without much change in the ground rules and administrative norms. The Indian politicians were still under the influence of the power elite and this set the stage for corruption and black money. The big business houses used their clout to influence political policy and agenda by directly exerting their control over political parties by providing funds for the electoral campaigns. They used their influence to also affect the bureaucratic appointments.

11. Black money is generated through a plethora of transactions and activities like misuse of public property payment of bribes, manipulation of expenses, misappropriation of public funds, evasion of taxes, etc.

12. The major causes of black money are corruption and crime, ineffective enforcement of tax laws, faulty social practices and norms, quota system, bribes, faulty taxation and laws, manipulation of accounts, illegal valuables and holdings, scarcity of resources, transfer activities, transactions through associate enterprises, inflation, real estate transactions, electoral funding and under-invoiced inventories.

1.6 QUESTIONS FOR REFLECTION

1. What are the basic connotations of black money?
2. List the characteristics of black money?
3. What are the sources of black money?
4. Why are tax havens so popular?
5. How has World War II affected the dynamics of black money?
6. List the major causes of black money?

Chapter 2

Indian Politics and Black Money

It is a well-known fact that Indian politics sits at the top of the ladder of black money. Black money and Indian politics go hand in hand. Politicians and political parties use the vehicle of elections to drive it by greasing its wheels with the fuel of black money. Black money is rampant at all levels of society—local and national governments, judicial wing, large and small businesses, executive functions, civil society and so on, but it is a major player in the political-corporate nexus. In the 2014 elections, the nexus between political parties and corporate houses was clearly visible. As far as electoral expenses are concerned, the 2014 elections were the most expensive elections fought ever.

Indian elections are a costly affair, but no one knows how costly they are. Electoral corruption in the form extortion, rigging and buying of votes, etc., leads to the generation of black money. Funding of political parties and the money spent during elections are the cause for political parties indulging in several black money practices like violation of ceiling amount, cash handouts, etc. Black money and its players need political muscle power to continue this vicious game. This muscle power corrupts the entire political, economic and social structure of the nation; it fosters anti-social elements. Due to this hand-in-glove relationship and corrupt political culture, premier investigation agencies of India like the Central Bureau of Investigation (CBI) and Central Vigilance Commission (CVC is an Indian governmental body that addresses governmental corruption) are not able to catch the black money criminals.

Most of the elections held so far have always revolved around corruption and black money dynamics. Black money in politics is cyclic in nature as it increases corruption, and this in turn leads to more generation of black money. This in turn affects not only the national reputation but also the international reputation of India. A corrupt political system tarnishes the global image of India. The Election Commission of India (EC is an autonomous constitutional authority responsible for administering the election processes in India) reported that during the Lok Sabha 2014 elections, around 300 crore rupees of unaccounted cash and more than 17,000 kgs of drugs and a huge amount of liquor, arms, etc., were seized [*Source*: Election Commission of India (http://eci.nic.in/eci/eci.html)].

The fight against black money in India is incomplete without fighting the corrupt practices in the sphere of Indian politics. Unless electoral funding is not brought under tax scrutiny, everything else that the Indian Government does in the name of the black money hunt will not succeed.

2.1 COLLUSION OF LAWMAKERS AND LAWBREAKERS

There is always collusion between the lawmakers and lawbreakers. Due to this collusion, the law and order scene in India is grim and the perpetrators get away scot-free every time. The real issue is not whether businessman A or businessman B are corrupt and indulge in black money hoarding, but whether the politicians, ministers, legislators, companies and people in the position of authority are corrupt or not. According to official statistics, one third of state and national legislators assume office with pending criminal charges. It is critical to ensure that Indian politicians who are caught in scams are brought to book.

Another aspect that is rampant when it comes to lawmakers/lawbreakers is that in the face of national crisis, they indulge in raising accusing fingers at each other without really wanting to deal with the real crisis. Public interest must get priority over narrow political agendas.

There have been numerous committees and commissions that have suggested several proposals for dealing with the various aspects of the black economy and many of their proposals have been implemented but in vain. The main reason for such failures is the collusion of lawmakers and lawbreakers. Election after election, we have witnessed the politicians morph from lawmakers to lawbreakers. As per the Indian law, those who are accused of crimes cannot be disbarred from contesting elections unless they are convicted. The irony of such a law is that most criminals get away due to the lack of solid evidence.

In the year 2016, members of the Indian Legislative Assembly had been booked on various charges including corruption and black money. According to Mr. N. Vittal (an Indian ex-civil servant and the Chief Vigilance Commissioner), "The basic principle in a democracy should be that a lawbreaker should not become a lawmaker, whether he is convicted for one year, six months, or five years. When lawmakers become lawbreakers or lawmakers collude with lawbreakers, the social stability is disturbed. Such disruptive behaviors need to be punished under the law; by strictly imposing punishment on these collusive factions, it will decrease the level of corruption as it will have deterrent effects." In an article titled: "Why voters elect criminals," Simon Chauchard, an Assistant Professor in the Government Department at Dartmouth College, writes: "Voters often preferred a criminal candidate from their own caste or party to a non-criminal candidate who was missing one of these attributes."

A Word of Caution

When lawmakers and lawbreakers become one, there is no doubt that the scope for generating black money increases. Widespread policy failure in India has led to the development and growth of the parallel economy. The collusion of lawmakers and lawbreakers has eroded the faith of the citizens in the state machinery. It is often seen that political pressure and connections help rich individuals and corporations to get away with their illegal activities.

Vote bank politics is a major reason for lawmakers turning into lawbreakers. Most political candidates offer free goods like wads of cash, alcohol and other questionable things in return for support and votes from voters. The politicians who are supposed to be honest lawmakers are themselves twisting the laws to suit their political agenda and they are always finding ingenious ways to fabricate their election expenditures and expense statements.

In September 2017, the investigative arm of the Income Tax Department found that the income and assets of the lawmakers were disproportionate with their known sources of income. Seven Lok Sabha Members of Parliament and 98 Members of Legislative Assembly were put under investigation for prima facie discrepancy between their assets and declared sources of income.

Good governance and electoral reforms are needed to free constituencies from the political domination of minority groups and also to encourage honest voters to come forward and vote for honest candidates. Good governance and electoral reforms are needed to ensure that the votes are not garnered based on divisive methods of religion and caste, but purely on the basis of merit and character. Good governance and electoral reforms cannot happen unless there is a fair and honest administration and political stability. With all these factors in place, only then the following equation can be wiped out from the black (money) board of the Indian landscape: Lawmakers + Lawbreakers = Black Money.

2.2 MONEY AND MUSCLE POWER IN POLITICS

The Election Commission (EC) aims to play an integral role in protecting the voters and voting apparatus from muscle power and also put a stranglehold over the money power. But all provisions and measures set up by the EC don't really deter politicians from exercising their political clout and muscle power. Politicians enjoy a God-given immunity whereas the common man has to face all the ups and downs of the wrongdoings of politicians. The Section 13A of the Income Tax Act, 1961, is what gives immunity to political parties in respect of their income from house property, other sources, capital gains and income by way of voluntary contributions received from any person. For this immunity to come into effect, they need to file their income tax returns to the Income Tax department within a time-based deadline, or else their accounts and incomes will be scrutinized. But in reality, the exact opposite scenario is happening; the political parties get to enjoy tax exemption and at the same time, they also get away from scrutiny using their muscle power.

Just as simple individuals and common man are thoroughly investigated; similarly, politicians and the source of funds of political parties need to be thoroughly investigated, and in the case of malpractices, they need to be punished. Stronger provisions and stricter implementation of such provisions are needed to keep a tab on political parties and their working, and all this should be done within a prescribed time-frame. Political funding is the main component of black money as it feeds and nurtures several other components of black money. The Indian Government needs to get rid of this double standard. If the common man bears the brunt, faces investigation, declares his income, answers questions, then political parties should undergo such serious scrutiny too. There should be no discrimination whatsoever.

Rather than declaring corporate funding of election campaigns as "unconstitutional," the Indian Government encourages the same. Only a few nations have managed to curb the corporate clout of interference, funding, donation and lobbying in policy-making. In India, there is a limit on what an individual candidate can spend, but there is no definite ceiling on what his or her political party can spend for general election campaign or where they can collect money for the same. The underreporting of expenditures by political candidates is a common phenomenon in Indian politics, and as of now there is no strict penalty in regards to the nondisclosure of such critical information. There is no accountability anywhere. All these factors facilitate more and more off-the-book contributions by the corporate world.

According to the analysis done by Association for Democratic Reforms (ADR is a non-partisan, non-governmental organization that works in the area of electoral and political reforms) and National Election Watch, 75 percent of the sources of funds to political parties remain unknown. According to yet another report compiled by ADR titled: 'Analysis of Income and Expenditure of National Political Parties for FY 2014-15', based on the income tax returns filed by the parties, the total income of political parties from unknown sources/mystery funding for the financial year 2014-15 was 685.36 crore rupees, which is approximately 54 percent of the total income of the parties. The unknown sources or mystery funding includes relief fund, sale of coupons, contributions from meetings, etc.

Table 2: % Share of Contributions in Total Income of Political Parties for FY 2014-15 (₹ in Crores)

Party	Total Income (A)	Source of Income	Total Contributions/ Donations (B)	Share of Contributions in Total Income (B/A)	Donations above 20,000 (C)	Share of Contributions above 20,000 (C/B)
BJP	970.43	Voluntary Contribution	872.02	90%	437.35	50%
BSP	111.955	Voluntary Contribution/ Coupon Sale	92.80	83%	0	0%
NCP	67.647	Grant/ Donation/ Contribution	38.82	57%	38.82	100%
CPI	1.84	Party Fund/ Election Fund/ Education Fund/ Donation	0.72	39%	1.33	185%
CPM	123.92	Voluntary Contribution	59.275	48%	3.419	6%
Grand Total	1,275,79		1,063.64	83%	480.92	45%

On the one hand, political parties have complained that the limits are too low, and on the other hand, the expenditure declared by them has been consistently well below the cap/limit (although in reality it is only on the higher side). In the 2014 Lok Sabha elections, the average election expenditure declared by the candidates was only ₹ 40.30 lakhs, which is approximately 59 percent of the limit imposed. These figures indicate blatant underreporting of election expenditures.

The limits that the Election Commission sets on election campaign expenditures and fund raising do not really satisfy the political parties; hence they look towards other means of meeting their over-the-top election funds. This is when they take a plunge in the dark waters of black money.

According to Section 182 of the Companies Act, 2013, no company in existence for less than three financial years can make a donation and the maximum amount that a company can contribute to a political party in a year should not exceed 7.5 percent of its average net profits during the three preceding financial years. But such acts and regulations are discarded by all black money game players. Several cases of fake companies donating large sums of money to political parties have been uncovered in the past few years.

It is a known fact that there is a significant influx of black money during poll time. Political parties raise funds to spend lakhs or perhaps crores of rupees for campaigning through billboards, advertisements, rallies, etc., but as their majority votes come from the masses, they use the black money portion of funds for distributing liquor, cigarettes and many other addictive things that are beyond the scope of this book.

The nexus of politics and black money is a big deterrent for sincere and honest people to enter into the field of politics. For keeping in line with the huge expenditures involved in electoral campaigns, politicians need to join hands with the world of black money. Politics attracts people who have a corrupt disposition and are willing to embezzle the national exchequer, and that is why honest, vigilant citizens are not interested in this dirty game of black money.

This nexus has yet another major downside. Politicians and political parties serve a dual purpose: the huge expenditures needed for their political rallies and campaigns are acquired from the black money investors/donors and at same time, these politicians provide the investors/donors the legitimacy to continue to generate more black money—a never-ending vicious cycle is created and set into motion. People are caught in a vicious never-ending cycle of the snake swallowing its own tail when they indulge in such rent-seeking activities like political lobbying by companies. This rent-seeking behavior is very dangerous for it has the potential to corrupt even the non-corrupt; if the rent-seeking behavior results in aggrandizement of wealth then there is a chance that anyone could enter into such transactions. In rent-seeking transactions, unless both parties believe they will benefit from the exchange, they will not consent. Several sectors like railways, mines, roads, etc., offer limitless opportunities to bring black money in the flow. Rent seeking is a type of economic behavior. Apart from big corporations, individual donors and industry giants playing this dirty game of black money on the pitch of politics, there is yet another player—independent candidates who pay excessive amounts of money to get tickets from political parties. Such expenditures are neither reflected in the financial accounts of political parties nor in the expenditure statements of individual candidates. This nondisclosure of sources of income and funding of political parties hampers the principles of accountability and transparency.

Politicians and political parties take all the constitutional procedures for granted. For example, despite of repeated notices from the Election Commission of India regarding electoral funding disclosure, politicians and political parties purposefully disclose these details very late as they know this also delays the investigation process conducted by the Election Commission. The more delayed the declaration, the more difficult it becomes to prove the malpractices. Research statistics regarding such undeclared assets is shocking: of the 3452 candidates who contested more than one election during the period from 2004 to 2013, 2967 showed an increase in wealth. The average declared wealth of such re-contesting candidates in 2004 was ₹ 1.74 crore rupees, and ₹ 4.08 crore rupees in 2013, an increase of 134 percent.

Though the recent demonetization drive of 2016 tried to kill two birds with one stone, both black money and political corruption, it did not achieve it fully. Some experts said that it was a bold move by the government in power, while others held the view that this move was nothing but a ploy to crush the opposition parties. Rather the *aam aadmi* (the common man) had to bear it all. This drive really did not adversely affect the political parties as they indulged in various tactics—they claimed that the money they got is all from small donors (cash donations less than ₹ 20,000 does not need any source; money for which there is no real source or income that is not taxed). It is not difficult for them to have created backdated donation receipts either. This defeated the entire purpose of this anti-black money operation.

> **A Word of Caution**
>
> There is no guarantee that a politician or political party that comes into power based on transparent funding will not indulge in corruption and black money.

2.2.1 Lobbying and Influence Peddling

Unlike the United States, lobbying is illegal in India. Corporate lobbying has become a necessary evil in current times. A popular example for rent-seeking is lobbying by the corporate world and companies in order to gain an advantage by influencing critical policy decisions that will work in their favor. Lobbyists and influence peddlers are basically people who use their tricks and tactics to influence government legislation agencies, appointments and schemes in their favor for their corporate clients. These lobbyists use various ways to influence political decisions and policies to gain special advantages and financial benefits at the cost of honest taxpayers, market competitors and consumers of their goods or services. Such 'black money' is increasing the inequalities in income leading to a new class of 'black' rich in a nation which is already stratified at many levels. In India, there is a powerful network of public relations firms that serve as corporate lobbyists for a wide variety of industries. Though lobbying is considered as illegal, but no nation in the world, including India has banned it. In fact, only a few nations even regulate lobbying practices, and these include nations like the United States and Australia.

The actual communication with politicians and government officials make up the smallest portion of lobbying. There are several other activities involved like information gathering, public relations campaigns, art of persuasion, etc., that also fall under the ambit of lobbying. The level of control and influence a lobbyist has over the politicians and legislative processes is usually directly proportional to the money and clout that a particular lobbyist possesses.

Often times, business players generate black money in order to meet certain expenses and costs that cannot be accounted for in the accounts books. Such expenses and costs include considerable political contributions, petty bribes to administrative officials, etc. It is this source of funding that the politicians do not want to disclose.

> **A Word of Caution**
>
> There is a popular opinion that people do not pay/evade taxes because the taxation levels are high. But many times, it is the source of income that is the primary reason for not paying/evading taxes. For example, political funding done through corporate donations.

Several credit card giants are said to be lobbying the Indian Government to ensure that they do not lose out their market share of the cashless economy during the digital payment push made by the Indian Government in order to introduce a cashless economy. Such giants are constantly lobbying with the government officials in order to protect their potential business and overcome any existential crisis, especially due to the presence of new digital payment avenues like Aadhaar Enabled Payment System (AEPS), Unified Payment Interface (UPI), BharatQR code and Bharat Interface for Money (BHIM).

There are several politicians who have stashed away their "lobby" loot in foreign locations and are operating the government machinery in a scot-free manner. In recent times, the Radia tapes demonstrated that the government, media, businessmen and several others have hand-in-glove equation with each other. Over a six-month period in 2009, the Indian Income Tax department taped Radia's phone conversations and the revelations were shocking. They showed how a small group of lobbyists, journalists, industrialists and politicians can fool the whole nation and influence the national policy. These taped conversations have also exposed how the political machinery functions as a crony of the corporate world. The Radia Tapes controversy clearly shows the gaps and grey areas in legislation; there is no legal provision that directly deals with malpractices in lobbying and public relations. Corporate lobbyists need to be brought under the scanner through a Lobbyist Act that requires all corporate lobbyists to register and report their financial activities and transactions. This is the first step in dealing with industrial houses that employ lobbyists to influence government policies for their own benefits. Canada's Lobbying Act and America's Lobbying Disclosure Act are good examples to follow.

After the Radia Tapes controversy, the Disclosure of Lobbying Activities (DLA) Bill was introduced in Lok Sabha in 2013. This Bill is a significant step because for the first time in the history of Indian lawmaking a potential law recognizes that lobbying is an integral part of democratic setup. It also stresses the need to create greater public awareness about lobbying activities in India. The Bill requires the Centre to set up a central authority for registration of lobbyists known as the Lobbyists' Registration Authority (LRA). This Bill covers lobbying activities intended to be undertaken by any entity, whether by itself or on behalf of others. It covers independent lobbying agencies, trade unions, non-profit groups as well as trade and business associations such as the Federation of Indian Chambers of Commerce and Industry (FICCI is the oldest and largest association of business organizations in India), which regularly represent their interests before the Indian Government. The LRA is the administrative authority under the DLA Bill which empowers it to conduct investigation probes against persons it suspects of having engaged in lobbying activities and practices without being registered with it. The provisions of the DLA do not apply retrospectively, which implies that the past cases of lobbying are not put under the scanner. Furthermore, the bill does not discuss in explicit terms as to how it is going to deal with foreign lobbyists engaged by Indian companies to lobby in India or abroad, or foreign lobbyists engaged by foreign companies to lobby in India.

In the year 2013, allegations against Walmart (Walmart is an American multinational company and the world's largest retailer) lobbying to get foreign direct investment (FDI) in multi-brand retail approved in India had created a huge furore in the Indian Parliament and in the nation as well. Walmart Stores was in the midst of an internal investigation over whether it had potentially violated the Foreign Corrupt Practices Act in India—suddenly found itself the target of bribery accusations by some of India's political leaders. "It has been officially confirmed that Walmart Company has indulged in lobbying in India, or in simple terms indulged in bribery," one party spokesman declared to the Indian press. Walmart Stores stated in a routine disclosure report to the Congress that it had spent 25 million dollars on lobbying activities in Washington over the past four years, including on issues related to "enhanced market access for investment in India". The uproar shut down Parliament operations for two days and forced the Indian Government to launch an inquiry to investigate these allegations that Walmart had bribed officials to gain access to India's profitable retail market. Walmart denied these allegations, stating that the lobbying had occurred with members of the United States Congress only and that too within the ambit of the US laws, and not with any Indian officials. This corporate controversy and political crises highlight just how differently the United States and India view and deal with the concept of lobbying.

According to the Section 182 of the Companies Act, 2013, no company in existence for less than three financial years can make a donation to a political party/electoral funding and that too within the given limit. Despite such laws, rules and regulations, there have been several cases where fake companies have donated huge amounts to political parties. The Section 29C of the Representation of People Act, 1951, mandates declaration of names of donors who have donated above 20,000 rupees. Due to this mandate, most of the political party funding remains anonymous. After several years, the Union Budget 2017 reduced the limit of cash donations to 2,000 rupees and all donations above that have to be declared. But such oversight provisions and legislations do not really deter political parties as they can use various tactics to conceal their funding; they can increase the number of donors donating 2,000 rupees or less in order to escape scrutiny.

The amendments to the Finance Bill 2017 have proposed to remove the following: the limit of 7.5 percent of net profit of the last three financial years, for contributions that a company may make to political parties; the requirement of a company to disclose the name of the political party to which a contribution has been made. Such amendments will definitely strengthen the political-corporate nexus. They will nullify the efforts to stop the channeling of black money into political parties.

Lobbying in India escapes the public eye due to the lack of regulation mechanisms and proper implementation of laws. It is not yet recognized in a statutory or non-statutory form in India, and this is a great cause for concern. A clear-cut definition and scope of lobbying and lobbying activities needs to be formulated. Currently, this definition is hazy; hence there are no clear-cut and comprehensive guidelines to deal with lobbying and its aspects of crony clientism and policy favoritism. The Radia Tapes controversy and the Walmart crisis was the first time when corporate lobbying became exposed in the public domain. To begin with a computerized repository containing all the details of the lobbyists, lobbied party/politician, financial activities and the policy being influenced should be maintained and updated by an independent body. All this information should be made available to the Indian public. The citizenry needs to be vigilant of which policies are being influenced because after all these lobbied policies have major effects on the welfare of the nation (mostly detrimental effects). The next important step is to ensure a fair democratic setup in order to facilitate the participation of citizens in the policy-making process. This public participation is necessary to keep a tab on unauthorized access by the corporate world to the policy-making process. Bringing citizens in the big picture through public participation and information sharing will make this whole process transparent and accountable. Also bringing all this information for media scrutiny would add to the transparency level. This approach needs to be implemented in spirit and only then it could possibly reduce harmful corporate lobbying activities, corruption and black money levels.

2.3 TOP-DOWN APPROACH AND GOOD GOVERNANCE AT ALL LEVELS

Unchecked power tends to become a corrupting force in any field, including politics and business. Political parties sit at the top of the ladder of black money. As everyone knows, politics is called the game of dirty money and hence it is critical that the political segment needs to be regulated and cleaned first. Finally the buck starts and stops with the politicians. Top leadership (of any country, including India) without integrity and accountability opens the door for the use of elected power to twist and turn the laws for personal gain and corporate gain.

In practice, political parties show only a small percentage of their actual income and raise the rest of their funding through various illegal means like selling of patronage and stealing from the national exchequer, and these means are not accounted for. One of the first steps towards making transparency a part of the political administration is making it mandatory for all parties to declare their incomes and expenditures at all levels (aggregated and disaggregated), right from the polling booth to the district level, and from the state level to the national level. Secondly every rupee should be traceable to the donor and using new technologies like real-time cloud reporting it can make it easier for achieving the desired level of responsibility, transparency and accountability. Such checks may or may not deter political parties and corporations from playing the dirty game of black money and corruption. But at least the transparency factor will make it difficult for the political-corporate nexus to get away with the wrongdoings.

Public participation is a critical component to bring about the top-down approach and good governance. This public participation should not be limited to only voting. It needs to expand to cover other aspects like rallies, protests, petitions, demonstrations, etc. Public assessment of the performance of their elected representatives provides feedback on the type of governance. A vigilant level of public participation in the political processes influences the micro and macro aspects of governance.

Another important factor of ensuring that there is clean politics top-down is that the politicians should be made accountable and answerable for all the economic gains. Only then these economic gains can be translated into the improvement of the economy in general and the society in particular. The administrative setup that works under the political setup needs to be cleaned up too. The administrative setup continues to misuse the controls and regulations still in place today to amass black money. These irrational controls and regulations need to go away.

The top-down approach for clean politics is a must but this needs to be mixed with the bottom-up element as well. Only when all the stakeholders of the political machinery and civil society participate in ensuring that the country's leadership acts with integrity then only good governance can be established at all levels. Political will at the topmost level is needed to push forward all positive policies and reforms and in turn, for this policies and reforms to work successfully, bottom-up support from the operational and middle levels of governance is needed.

2.3.1 Clean From the Top

"Jhadu uppar se lagai jaati hai" is a Hindi proverb, which essentially means if one really wants to clean one's house, one should start cleaning from the top. The same principle applies to the process of cleaning up of black money. Cleaning up of black money is like cleaning stairs; one must start at the top and work one's way down. Another aspect of cleaning from the top includes tackling the menace from the inside. The focus should shift from too much dependence on external agencies to cleaning up of various government wings and departments from within the setup.

Politicians at the top of the black money ladder are able to carry out their spurious activities by virtue of help coming from the web of other supportive (unethical) players like corporates, lawyers, accountants, banks, public servants, and many more. This complex web of players needs to be cleaned up in a top-down manner and the election machinery needs to be put under strict vigilance. In order for this cleanup to be successful, a clear view of 'the under the table dynamics' is necessary; we have discussed several aspects of these dynamics up until this point and will continue to unearth more aspects in the upcoming sections and chapters as well. Black money needs to be mopped up by starting to make political funding transparent and accountable. Yes the cleanup starts from way up there but needs to continue down each and every step of the way.

Spotlight

The past several decades have exposed so many political scandals that have involved black money and corruption. Each politician is a parallel economy unto herself/himself. To overcome this political apathy towards the nation and its citizens, India needs systemic reforms to curtail political involvement in the generation of black money. Politicians need to be made accountable to their voters, their citizens and civil society of the country, as they are the ones who put them up there on that political pedestal.

The citizenry should also play a vigilant role in this cleanup operation. They should cast their votes only in a clean election. Only when all parties voluntarily and mandatorily declare their expenses, then the voters can and should think of casting their votes. Again the declarations by politicians should be open to challenge by the Election Commission, civil society and the public.

The Indian Government launched the 'Operation Clean Money' in 2017. The aim of this online portal is to bring illegal wealth on books; another step in the fight against black money. It was launched to create awareness about black money and to e-verify large cash deposits made during the period from 9th November to 30th December 2016. Its main aims are to facilitate transparent tax administration, enable citizen engagement to improve tax compliance and appropriate enforcement action. More such initiatives and portals should be launched to bring more and more tax evaders, including the top brass of the political and corporate worlds, under the scanner.

2.3.2 Good Governance is a Must

Good governance means the exercise of political, economic and administrative authority for the common good. The political leadership needs to provide economic stability, protection and public services to the Indians. To end the marriage of politics and black money, the Indian Government has to do more than demonetization. Over the past several decades, due to the controlled economy in India, there has been a parallel economy of black money running alongside. Many corporations, both small and large, have indulged in amassing black money through black channels.

> **Spotlight**
>
> Rather than adopting imported models of corporate governance blindly, India needs to pick out the best provisions from these foreign models and then add to or modify the existing provisions to adapt to the local context.

Apart from the political players showing a strong political will to put an end to the menace of black money, the corporate players also need to play a responsible role in curbing the menace of black money. It is time for the corporate captains to put forth a good corporate governance code to ensure equality and fairness for all the stakeholders involved, including their customers.

Political parties should realize that the fight against black money is not solely a political fight, but rather should be a collective effort by all political parties (ruling and opposition); this fight should be kept above intra-party politics and inter-party politics. Political governance is needed for protecting the interests of the public through sound policies. It is about being sensitive and responsive to the needs of the people, and not indulging in populism at all. Everyone should be given equal opportunity. Only when politicians set an example of honest living, only then will the citizens follow in their footsteps. Good governance also translates into the ability of the citizens to effectively take part in the choice of their elected representatives and to effectively participate in the decisions made on issues that affect them.

Good governance will lead to an increase in tax revenues. This increase is good if the money is being utilized for the welfare of the people. The same increase is harmful if revenues are being utilized for filling up the coffers of politicians. Politicians need to develop a responsible attitude towards their positions and deliver citizen-centric services by leveraging e-governance tools in order to deliver these services in a time-bound manner.

Good political governance essentially requires active participation of different sectors of the society. Active participation refers to active involvement of all affected and interested parties in the decision-making process for all aspects, including the fight against black money. It requires an enabling environment whereby relevant data, statistics and information are disseminated and people are allowed to respond in a free manner. It is about the Indian politicians and government machinery working hand-in-hand with other sectors of the civil society. A major aspect missing in setting up good political governance is that the gap between the election promises and resulting performance is never considered; mostly all these political promises are calendar fodder. This gap needs to be studied and any failure on the part of politicians needs public scrutiny. This is needed to establish accountability and responsibility among politicians.

Just like a nation needs the support of the three main pillars/ wings of legislature, executive and judiciary to run smoothly so does any corporation need the support of the four pillars in terms of management, board of directors, regulators and auditors. These four pillars need to work in unison to implement a strict corporate governance code and encourage ethical behaviors at all levels. But in reality, the exact opposite is witnessed: these four pillars tend to play the "blame game". Rather than playing this blame game, companies should be serious about tackling tax evasion and avoidance, hence the corporate world needs to rethink about the ways these companies are allowed to be operated.

In India, corporate governance is not that strictly implemented; it is mostly on paper. It is generally seen that the management is callous in their attitude. The board of directors only cares for its share of power and monetary returns. It is essential to ensure that the dominant shareholders do not exploit the minority shareholders. As far as oversight of management is concerned, the board members should be absolutely strict, but when it comes to dominant shareholders, the board members become helpless because that is where they get their power from. Hence strict implementation of corporate governance is a must for establishing a culture of equitability, discipline, transparency, consensus and accountability whereby malpractices can be minimized. Regulating the corporate world is of utmost importance for keeping a tab on illegal political funding and lobbying practices, and also for improving tax compliance. The need of the hour is to create a strong administrative system.

The management should walk the talk and should set an example of honesty for their employees and other stakeholders to follow. The board of directors should play their role of ensuring the company's growth by collectively directing the company's working, whilst meeting the interests of its shareholders, stakeholders and customers, and also ensuring only fair corporate practices are followed. Especially in the case of independent directors, who are more interested in commissions and fees, the corporate governance strategy should include strong policy deterrence measures.

There are many provisions in the Indian Companies Act to penalize corporate miscreants, but somehow they manage to get away each time they are caught. Corporate governance under the new Indian Companies Act, 2013, has broadened its meaning to meet the challenges of the present-day corporate world. The broadened meaning and context include provisions related to the composition of the board, admittance of women directors, internal audit, and several other parameters. Despite these detailed provisions, corporate criminals still get away and this is due to the lack of implementing these provisions, or they are abused or misused. Auditors of the corporations need to be under the scanner as they are the ones who report lapses, misrepresentations or violations that lead to the generation of black money. The Indian Companies Act does have provisions for this aspect, but strict implementation of the same is a must to hold the auditors responsible and accountable for such lapses. Such a strict environment will help honest auditors to come forward and report all these violations without any fear of being marginalized or silenced.

Banks and financial institutions need to play a more vigilant role in order to support the good corporate governance aspect. They need to play an active role in monitoring transactions and be strict when it comes to reporting of shady transactions to the authorities.

In some foreign nations, tax compliance is a key component that determines the level of corporate governance. The inclusion of tax compliance in corporate governance programmes should be stipulated by the Indian Government under various provisions of the law. On the one hand, corporations show support towards anti-black money measures such as the demonetization drive of 2016, but on the other hand, they also engage in a lot of complex activities of converting their black money into white. They should have supported this drive in full spirit and all honesty to uphold the principles of corporate governance and transparency.

Corporate governance in the banking sector is equally critical as banks are pivotal to the economic stability of India, and for that matter any other nation too. Corporate governance is necessary for banks to keep an eye on illegal transactions, corrupt dealings and money laundering. A combination of technology-based transaction tracking and actionable intelligence should be used by banks, companies and authorities at all levels in order to implement a good and successful governance strategy.

In September 2017, the Indian Government's Ministry of Finance implemented stricter norms of corporate governance. It was decided that in case the director or authorized signatory of any struck off company tried to siphon-off money from the bank account/s in an unauthorized manner, s/he may get imprisonment of not less than six months and it can be extended to 10 years. It was decided that the directors of such shell companies which have not filed their returns for three or more years will be disqualified from being appointed in any other company as a director or from being reappointed as a director in any of the previous companies where they had been a director. The Indian Government has also taken this one step further by putting efforts to identify the actual beneficiaries and other people like company secretaries, cost accountants, chartered accountants, etc., behind the operations of such shell companies, and have put all of these entities under the scanner. All the banks are given strict instructions to keep a tab on all the accounts and transactions of such struck off companies. All these new measures are implemented for protecting the interests of the stakeholders, for promoting a fair business climate, and for choking the availability of funds for illegal purposes.

Spotlight

Tax evasion, corruption, illicit financial flows and poor governance all are interlinked. To replace the poor governance with good governance, we need better tools of governance and a better system of enforcement of laws. This is necessary for guaranteeing the fundamental rights of the sincere and honest elements of the society. Once the good governance component is in place, the three negatives of tax evasion, corruption and illicit financial flows can be kept under control.

2.4 CHAPTER RECAP

1. It is a well-known fact that Indian politics sits at the top of the ladder of black money. Black money and Indian politics go hand in hand. Politicians and political parties use the vehicle of elections to drive it by greasing its wheels with the fuel of black money.

2. Black money is rampant at all levels of society—local and national governments, judicial wing, large and small businesses, executive functions, civil society and so on, but it is a major player in the political-corporate nexus. In the 2014 elections, the nexus between political parties and corporate houses was clearly visible. As far as electoral expenses are concerned, the 2014 elections were the most expensive elections fought ever.

3. The fight against black money in India is incomplete without fighting the corrupt practices in the sphere of Indian politics. Unless electoral funding is not brought under tax scrutiny, everything else that the Indian Government does in the name of the black money hunt will not succeed.

4. According to official statistics, one third of state and national legislators assume office with pending criminal charges. It is critical to ensure that Indian politicians who are caught in scams are brought to book.

5. There have been numerous committees and commissions that have suggested several proposals for dealing with the various aspects of the black economy and many of their proposals have been implemented but in vain. The main reason for such failures is the collusion of lawmakers and lawbreakers. Election after election, we have witnessed the politicians morph from lawmakers to lawbreakers. As per the Indian law, those who are accused of crimes cannot be disbarred from contesting elections unless they are convicted. The irony of such a law is that most criminals get away due to the lack of solid evidence.

6. Vote bank politics is a major reason for lawmakers turning into lawbreakers. Most political candidates offer free goods like wads of cash, alcohol and other questionable things in return for support and votes from voters. The politicians who are supposed to be honest lawmakers are themselves twisting the laws to suit their political agenda and they are always finding ingenious ways to fabricate their election expenditures and expense statements.

7. Good governance and electoral reforms are needed to free constituencies from the political domination of minority groups and also to encourage honest voters to come forward and vote for honest candidates.

8. Just as simple individuals and common man are thoroughly investigated; similarly, politicians and the source of funds of political parties need to be thoroughly investigated, and in the case of malpractices, they need to be punished.

9. According to the analysis done by Association for Democratic Reforms (ADR is a non-partisan, non-governmental

organization that works in the area of electoral and political reforms) and National Election Watch, 75 percent of the sources of funds to political parties remain unknown.

10. Politicians and political parties serve a dual purpose: the huge expenditures needed for their political rallies and campaigns are acquired from the black money investors/donors and at same time, these politicians provide the investors/donors the legitimacy to continue to generate more black money—a never-ending vicious cycle is created and set into motion.

11. Unlike the United States, lobbying is illegal in India. A popular example for rent-seeking is political lobbying by the corporate world and companies in order to gain an advantage by influencing critical policy decisions that will work in their favor. Lobbyists are basically people who use their tricks and tactics to influence government legislation and agencies in their favor for their corporate clients.

12. The actual communication with politicians and government officials make up the smallest portion of lobbying. There are several other activities involved like information gathering, public relations campaigns, etc., that also fall under the ambit of lobbying. The level of control and influence a lobbyist has over the politicians and legislative processes is usually directly proportional to the money and clout that a particular lobbyist possesses.

13. After the Radia Tapes controversy, the Disclosure of Lobbying Activities (DLA) Bill was introduced in Lok Sabha in 2013. This Bill is a significant step because for the first time in the history of Indian lawmaking a potential law recognizes that lobbying is an integral part of democratic setup. It also stresses the need to create greater public awareness about lobbying activities in India. The Bill requires the Centre to set up a central authority for registration of lobbyists known as the Lobbyists' Registration Authority (LRA).

14. Top leadership (of any country, including India) without integrity and accountability opens the door for the use of elected power to twist and turn the laws for personal gain and corporate gain.

15. One of the first steps towards making transparency a part of political administration is making it mandatory for all parties to declare their incomes and expenditures at all levels (aggregated and disaggregated), right from the polling booth to the district level, and from the state level to the national level.

16. Public participation is a critical component to bring about the top-down approach and good governance. This public participation should not be limited to only voting. It needs to expand to cover other aspects like rallies, protests, petitions, demonstrations, etc. Public assessment of the performance of their elected representatives provides feedback on the type of governance. A vigilant level of public participation in the political processes influences the micro and macro aspects of governance.

17. The top-down approach for clean politics is a must but this needs to be mixed with the bottom-up element as well. Only when all the stakeholders of the political machinery and civil society participate in ensuring that the country's leadership acts with integrity then only good governance can be established at all levels. Political will at the topmost level is needed to push forward all positive policies and reforms and in turn, for this policies and reforms to work successfully, bottom-up support from the operational and middle levels of governance is needed.

18. Good governance means the exercise of political, economic and administrative authority for the common good. The political leadership needs to provide economic stability, protection and public services to the Indians.

19. Apart from the political players showing a strong political will to put an end to the menace of black money, the corporate players also need to play a responsible role in curbing the menace of black money. It is time for the corporate captains to put forth a good corporate governance code to ensure equality and fairness for all the stakeholders involved, including their customers.

20. Just like a nation needs the support of the three main pillars/wings of legislature, executive and judiciary to run smoothly so does any corporation need the support of the four pillars in terms of management, board of directors, regulators and auditors.

21. Banks and financial institutions need to play a more vigilant role in order to support the good corporate governance aspect. They need to play an active role in monitoring transactions and be strict when it comes to reporting of shady transactions to the authorities.

2.5 QUESTIONS FOR REFLECTION

1. How does politics affect the dynamics of black money?
2. What is lobbying?
3. How do governance, corruption and tax evasion link up?
4. Is transparency in lobbying the silver bullet for controlling black money?
5. What is the significance of corporate governance?
6. How can political governance support the civil society?
7. How does electoral funding affect the fabric of the society?
8. Should lobbying be treated as a legitimate activity in India?
9. What are the components of good governance?

PART 2

Magnitude of Black Money and Its Reach in India

Chapter 3

Magnitude is Immense and Many Players are Involved

During the colonial era, as far back as 1936, the Ayers Committee was set up to investigate and evaluate the income tax administration in India, and it also suggested large-scale amendments to secure the interests of the honest taxpayers and effectively deal with fraudulent elements. As black money transactions are mainly cash-based and moreover, all the players involved go to extra lengths to cover their tracks, data sources and economic methods tend to come up with rough or understated estimates. At the economic summit of 2000, the then Central Vigilance Commissioner estimated that black money accounted for 40 percent of GDP. According to statistics, 14,000 crore rupees is the money held by Indians in Swiss banks as of December 2013, a jump of over 42 percent from 2012. Such glaring statistics call for some serious measures. Over the last several years, the Indian Government has set up numerous committees and study groups to study and report on the problem of black money, and also to suggest measures. Some of the notable committees and study groups include: Wanchoo Committee also known as the Direct Taxes Enquiry Committee—report on tax evasion and black money (1971), Dangli Committee on Controls and Subsidies (1980), National Institute of Public Finance and Policy report (Aspects of the Black Economy in India, 1985), White Paper on Black Money (2012) and many more.

Table 3: Black Money Estimates in India

	Year/ Period	Amount (billion dollars)	% of Gross Domestic Product
Domestic Tax Evaded Income			
Wanchoo Committee	1961	8	4.5
Mr. O.P. Chopra (Prominent Economist)	1977	81	8.7
National Institute of Public Finance and Policy	1984	316-368	19-21
World Bank	2007	9019	21
Offshore Black Money			
IMF and later revisions	1971-1997	4400	31
Swiss National Bank	2012	90	0.1
Global Financial Integrity			
Estimate Flight of Capital	1947-2010	11.6	17.9
Estimate of Illicit Assets	2010	24350	37.6

Table Source: Jeffries May 2014 Report on VDIS (Jefferies India Pvt. Ltd., a prominent Foreign Financial Institution)

In 2011, Corruption Perception Index ranked India at position 94 among 176 countries with a score of 36, and this score shows that India faces a serious problem. Global Financial Integrity (GFI) in its report 'Illicit Financial Flows to and from Developing Countries: 2005-2014' stated that 101 billion dollars black money entered India while 23 billion dollars exited from the nation. Another report found six of the top fifteen exporters of illicit financial flows/capital are Asian countries: India, Thailand, China, the Philippines, Malaysia and Indonesia. GFI research also revealed that international corporate entities have a major hand behind the illicit financial flows. Traded misinvoicing carried out by multinational corporations make up about 80 percent of illicit financial flows worldwide. Traded misinvoicing is a method for moving large amounts of money illicitly across borders which involves fraudulent trade transactions; this is done using methods of under-invoicing and over-invoicing where the value of a transaction is misrepresented or misreported. The Wanchoo Committee Report (Government of India, Ministry of

Finance, 1971, p. 6) stated that the phenomenon of black of money is a "cancerous growth in the country's economy which, if not checked in time, will surely lead to its ruination". And this is exactly what has transpired in the last 40+ years. A study by the Centre for Monitoring Indian Economics (CMIE is a leading think tank that provides services to governments, academia, businesses, etc.) found in 2006 that each parliamentary poll generates between 10.19 billion dollars and 11.33 billion dollars of black money. According to studies, 1.1 trillion dollars flowed illicitly out of developing and emerging economies in 2013 alone, and this is a dramatic increase since the year 2004, when illicit outflows were pegged at just 465.3 billion dollars.

When a patient visits a doctor for a checkup and medicines, and then pays two thousand rupees without a bill, it becomes black money. When the same doctor goes to a posh restaurant and spends it on dinner, it is billed and it becomes white again, but the doctor hid his income. Such small instances across sectors make bigger and bigger ripples, and the biggest ripples are caused by major players like politicians, corporates, bureaucrats, etc. Several factors contribute to this growing magnitude of illicit financial flows across the borders. Some of the main factors are abuse of political power, secrecy jurisdictions and tax havens, abuse of tax structure and regulatory frameworks, corruption, criminal activities, etc. These factors offer wealthy individuals and powerful corporations to move their money and assets globally without much hindrance.

3.1 FROM POLITICS TO ECONOMY

Experts believe that if all the money in the underground economy could be diverted to the main Indian economy, then the economy would grow by more than thrice in no time. We have already seen the detrimental effects of the nexus between politics and black money on India in the previous chapter. According to recent statistics, India ranks at the 8th position among 150 other countries that have the highest amount of black money. This alarming rank clearly shows the lack of political will to change things for the better. The cash outflow from the main economy towards the black, parallel economy adversely affects various sectors of the economy including education and healthcare. According to a study by the Global Financial Integrity (GFI), for India, the average annual illicit outflow for the years 2008-12 was 4 percent of GDP, 10 percent of trade, 215 percent of foreign direct investment, nearly 120 percent of the government's annual education expenditure, about 100 percent of the government's annual health expenditure, 40 percent of total tax revenue and 0.7 percent of capital stock.

Table 4: Cash Outflow: Yearly Black Money Outflows as % of Various Parameters

GDP	4
Trade	10
FDI (Foreign Direct Investment)	215
Education Spend	119
Health Spend	101
Total Tax Revenues	40

Source: GFI Report June 2015; Data for 2008-12

Now it is time to focus on the 'economy' aspect of India. The first term that comes to mind is parallel economy. Such an economy has hampered true economic development of this nation and has squashed the dreams of sincere, hardworking people. Another aspect is that the national exchequer faces a huge loss in terms of tax evasion; hence there is a gap between public resources and public welfare expenditures, and this affects the overall growth of the economy and the quality of living too. Also to meet this gap, the Indian Government attempts to raise more indirect taxes, which leads to a higher incidence of tax on the poor and middle classes, and this in turn erodes mass demand levels. To fill the gap caused by tax evasion, the Indian Government has to resort to high taxation and the burden of this high taxation falls on sincere, honest taxpayers.

Another measure that the Indian Government resorts to fill this deficit is through deficit financing. Deficit financing is a method of meeting government budgetary deficits through public loans and creation of new money. When public investment is financed by borrowing rather than by taxation, this kind of borrowing is called deficit financing. This method has a set of advantages: creating additional employment, handling the period of depression, and financing economic development. This method has a set of disadvantages too that impact the economy: it leads to inflation and this in turn leads to an increase in credit creation by banks, it adversely affects the distribution of income and resources as the business and industrial classes benefit and profit from the rise in prices and become more richer, and finally inflation also increases the level of corruption. The disadvantages far outweigh the advantages. The honest class has to bear the brunt of high taxes in order to fill up the deficit caused by tax evasion done by the rich class.

A Word of Caution

It is possible to convert black money through various means, which is the main character of the illegal economy. There are several techniques of converting black money into white money and vice versa, and thereby the perpetrators of such conversion get away from being caught. This dynamic behavior of black money has led to the creation of yet another class of 'black' rich in an economy and a society which is already so deeply entrenched in stratification and class system.

The outflow of black money (that should be actually pumped or invested back in India) causes the economic conditions to deteriorate further. The involvement of black money in public sector projects affects the quality of these projects and moreover leads to underhand dealings through kickbacks and tender manipulations. Several rich and successful Indian businessmen have acquired the non-resident Indian status and this helps them to evade taxes, and this evasion leads to less resources being pumped back into the Indian economy. According to New World Wealth (New World Wealth is a global market research group), India saw the fourth biggest outflow of uber-rich individuals globally in 2015 with 4,000 millionaires changing their domicile by moving abroad. This figure went up to approximately 6,000 millionaires in 2016.

Policy paralysis is a huge factor in thwarting the growth of the Indian economy. Loans to sectors and industries that have graft problems are like a tight slap on the face of the Indian economy. Scams like the 2G Spectrum, Coalgate, and various others also have adversely affected the Indian economy. Other nations that have seen such a major outflow of high net worth individuals are China, France and Brazil.

The main players of the Indian economy, i.e., the uber-rich class, are getting richer at a faster pace. According to the latest data on global wealth shared by Credit Suisse Group AG (a Swiss multinational financial services holding company), the richest one percent of Indians now own 58.4 percent of the country's wealth. According to the Household Survey on India's Citizen Environment and Consumer Economy report conducted in 2016, the average monthly household income of the richest one percent of Indians is 66,627 rupees and that of the richest 10 percent is 35,605 rupees. But again these figures are far too understated as they are based on self-reported data; these are all soft estimates. The presence of a large parallel, underground economy leads to such underestimation and presents an inaccurate picture of the economy. Accurate calculation of GDP (gross domestic product), imports and exports, sector-wise composition of national income, savings-to-income ratio and other measures is not possible; hence the correct assessment of the health of the country's economy does not happen. Such underestimated figures also affect policy-making. One thing is for sure that these figures and statistics show how lop-sided the Indian economy is and how only one segment is prospering at the cost of other segments. Black money makes the rich richer and the poor poorer thereby causing regressive distribution of income and wealth. This leads to concentration of money, wealth and assets in the hands of a few. Black money creates social tension between the haves and have-nots.

The nouveau riche class is over ambitious in their plans; hence they resort to all types of unethical means to make a quick buck. The inequality of income caused by black money also affects the distribution of scarce resources. The rich are able to buy such resources because of their readiness and ability to pay and this in turn, deprives the honest class from having access to such resources. Black money makes it difficult for ordinary people to survive. The higher capacity to pay of the rich class also hampers middle and lower classes from realizing their dream of having a home. The rich and super rich with their deep pockets are ready to pay any amount for a piece of land, and due to this the prices of the surrounding land pieces also tend to increase. This causes artificial inflation of prices in an entire area or neighborhood. Moreover, as most of the upper segment is involved in black money in one way or the other, it is ready to invest any amount of money in real estate and property as this helps to convert black money into white, legal money.

The abolition of the Gift Tax Act has encouraged black money hoarders and racketeers to generate more and more unaccounted money. The Gift Tax Act, constituted in the year 1958, stated that all gifts in excess of ₹ 50,000, in the form of cash, draft, movable or immovable assets, jewelry, check or others, received from one (donor) who does not have any blood relation with the recipient, were taxable. In 1998, this act was abolished as a tax relief measure for middle class taxpayers who gave and received gifts. Due to this abolishment, both the donor and recipient did not have to pay any tax on the gifts. This led to a lot of misuse in terms of businesses creating black money, gifts transferred from non-relatives and benami properties. To overcome such gaps, in 2004, the Gift Tax Act was again renewed partially under Income from Other Sources, with the Section 56(2)(vi) of the Income Tax Act being passed in 2004. The gift tax is applicable to any amount exceeding 50,000 rupees obtained by a person or a Hindu Undivided Family (According to Hindu Law, HUF is a family which consists of all persons lineally descended from a common ancestor) without any consideration from any person would be taxed under the head 'Income from Other Sources'. This section also states under what conditions the gift tax will not be applicable: from any relative; or on the occasion of marriage of the individual; or any person under a will or by way of inheritance; or any person in contemplation of death of the payer; or any trust registered under Section 12AA; or any institution or trust referred to in Section 10(23).

Black money also affects the quality of various public schemes and programs. It increases the economic costs of such government projects. The constant generation of black money makes fewer funds available for such infrastructure projects and social schemes for the poor and downtrodden; hence they adversely affect the welfare of the public. Black money thwarts the flow of the resources in the right direction.

3.2 BLACK MONEY ON ITS WAY TO BANKS

Politicians and businessmen swindle huge funds from banks. Moreover, several of these bank funds and loans are diverted for other purposes than the official purposes for which they have been granted.

Modern-day banking needs technology to process its transactions. During the 2016 demonetization drive, banks should have played a more proactive and intensive role in using technology tools to nab the black marketers and tax evaders. In certain cases, the exact opposite scenario was witnessed; officials of some of the private sector banks were alleged to have helped those with black money to launder funds during the demonetization drive.

According to statistics by the Global Financial Integrity (GFI), counterfeit money deposited into non-Indian banks by the Indian politicians, businessmen and celebrities since 1991 pegs at a whopping 2,100,000 crore rupees. This is where the concept of tax havens comes into picture. Another statistics by the GFI states that Indian economy has lost its money ranging from 450 billion dollars to 1,500 billion dollars on account of black money flows into banks in foreign nations. Credit Suisse and USB banks account for nearly two-third of the total money kept by foreigners in Swiss banks and their share in the case of Indians is even higher at approximately 82 percent. Also the US and the UK have large sums in these banks.

Switzerland has recently given a green signal for automatic exchange of financial account information (AEI) with India. India will be able to access all the transactions between Indians and Swiss banks from 2019 onwards, but this ‘delay’ time window will give black money account holders plenty of time to move their illegal money to other tax havens in order to avoid their information being shared with the Indian Government. One major loophole of this agreement is that it will only involve sharing of information about bank account holders from 2018 onwards. This loophole defeats the very purpose of AEI and it will also give an unreal picture of these black money accounts.

More than 1,50,000 offshore corporations are formed each year (Hines, J.R., Jr. and E.M. Rice, 1994, "Fiscal Paradise: Foreign Tax Havens and American Business" *Quarterly Journal of Economics*).

In 2009, Germany handed over a list of Indian account holders in LGT Bank, Liechtenstein. In 2011, France handed over a list of 782 Indians who supposedly hold HSBC accounts in Geneva. There is so much information that the Indian Government had in regards to black money hoarders, but there is lack of concerted efforts from the authorities to do something concrete against such lists. By just recovering a few million dollars of stashed away cash, we cannot expect to see the Indian horizon cleared off of the air of black money; hoarders, fraudsters and defaulters need to be brought to book immediately.

Spotlight

As per the data and statistics of 2014, the total money in Swiss banks is 1,776 million Swiss francs held directly by Indian individuals and entities and 38 million Swiss francs held through wealth managers.

As per the estimates revealed by the Swiss National Bank, the total amount of money held in Swiss banks by foreign clients from across the world increased from 1.41 trillion Swiss francs to 1.42 trillion Swiss francs during 2016. The funds parked in Swiss banks from offshore financial centers increased to 389 billion Swiss francs. India was ranked 61 in 2015 and 75 in 2016. India was ranked highest at position 37 in the year 2004.

Table 5: Swiss Bank Money List Ranking

Rank	Country	Money (in Swiss Franc)
1	United Kingdom	350 billion
2	United States	196 billion
17	Russia	17.6 billion
28	China	7.4 billion
69	Pakistan	1.5 billion
75	India	1.2 billion

Though not every penny parked in the Swiss Banks by Indians is black, yet a considerable amount of it is not reported for and falls in the category of black money. According to the latest statistics, India has moved down to the 61st place in terms of foreigners' money in Swiss banks. But this does not mean that the black money level has decreased rather Indians have become more cautious when it comes to parking their money in Swiss Banks. They have found other ways of doing this, by moving their funds to other tax havens; therefore, the decline in deposits does not indicate a decline in black money. After India's recent information exchange deal with Switzerland that will come into effect from 2019, more Indians are likely to shift their illegal money from Swiss bank accounts to other safer offshore locations. It is highly likely that by the time this treaty comes into effect, there would be hardly any accounts left to be scrutinized.

In 2014, as much as three-fifths of India's total gold imports came from Switzerland; India imported 471.9 tons of gold from Switzerland. This was done by over-invoicing the gold imports from Switzerland, which helped them to bring back the black money as white money into the nation. Rich Indians also use other channels like property and foreign direct investment for bringing back the money into the legal, white money economy.

Banks need to play a more vigilant role in tracing all money transactions and pinpointing financial frauds with the proper backing of technology. Using various analysis tools and latest technology trends, both at the input and supply points, banks can monitor the money trail, identity, cash flow, account details, inter-account transfers, denomination involved, etc., to capture and report all types of monetary malpractices. Cash counting machines should be made compulsory in the banking sector to locate anomalies in the transactions. It is necessary for banks to carry out cash flow process in a vigilant manner in order to improve their surveillance and detection mechanisms. The strict implementation of a transparency and rules-based system throughout the banking sector will at least help to curb the circulation in the nation. CCTV footage is a must for keeping a watch over all the activities and movements within the premises.

Income Tax department, Enforcement Directorate and Central Bureau of Investigation should conduct regular searches of various banks across India to keep a tab on their functioning and to spot if there are any suspicious transactions. The Indian Government and its investigating agencies should not wait for any specific demonetization drive or any other measure to carry out their duties of vigilance and surveillance. Suspicious safe deposit boxes also need to be checked and this includes safe deposit services run by private operators too.

Many land-owners do not grow crops on their land; they use their land for different purposes. However, after the demonetization of 2016, they showed the source of their incomes as the sale of produce/crops at a higher price. However, these transactions existed only in books. In this way, these land-owners managed to deposit their black money without coming under the lens of scrutiny. The banks, too, did not bother to verify such claims.

The unaccounted money held in foreign bank accounts generated through hawala deals needs to be put under strict investigation and under the lens of the national and international investigating agencies. Even local banks need to be put under the lens to capture any money laundering-related activities. During the demonetization drive of 2016, it was alleged that several banks helped black money holders who had accounts in these banks to launder their money and also the Central Bureau of Intelligence was pursuing leads in this regards. Several bank officials became money agents wherein they helped people to change old notes into new notes directly or through their family, friends and other types of illegal couriers, and every person involved in such conversions received a commission.

3.3 GROUND REALITIES AND EFFECTS SINCE DEMONETIZATION OF 2016

Withdrawing of high denomination currency notes has been done before in 1946 and in 1978, and now in the recent past it was initiated in November 2016. The Indian Government undertook demonetization on November 8, 2016. Social media and news channels have been filled with public frenzy, stories and reactions in relation to this currency purge right from day one since its announcement. Without future, well-thought policy changes, the current short-term benefits of this drive are bound to run out soon. As the problem of unaccounted money and wealth is much bigger and is not just limited to hoarding of money, demonetization in itself will have only a limited impact and that too only for a short while.

Earlier, high tax rates were considered a major source of black money in India. Now, India has moved to a low tax regime. Yet, low tax rates and new reforms are not adequate and will not address the problem of black money completely. Hence, demonetization can and may provide additional relief. But demonetization alone cannot be a complete success in itself. In the recent demonetization drive, pulling out 500 and 1,000 notes from circulation and then the decision to print new 2,000 rupee notes was not a wise step, as it has aggravated the problem of black money. A more balanced way would have been to allow small denominations up to ₹ 100 accompanied by a mechanism to propagate the wider use of debit/credit cards in place of currency.

Post-demonetization, the unorganized sector was severely hit by the demonetization-driven cash crunch. The rich and elite have always enjoyed and will continue to enjoy their vast hoardings, majorly in the form of offshore assets, foreign bank accounts, trusts, property and gold, and in a limited form of cash.

According to 2014 industry research of the banking sector, "A combination of negative interest rates (adjusted for inflation) and a boom in real estate and gold induced savers to increase investments in property and gold and cut down on their exposure to bank deposits and equity markets. This choked the flow of funds to banks and the capital market, making it tough for firms to raise capital" (Devendra Patil, head economist at India Ratings, was quoted in *Business Standard*, May 31, 2014). Two years later in 2016, the banking situation had become worse with declining profits and increasing bad debts. The demonetization drive of 2016 was launched with a dual purpose in mind: to curb black money and to save the assets of the banking sector. While there is some benefit in the form of unclaimed balances and potential tax revenue, but to declare that this move will terminate the circulation of black money is a far away dream.

3.3.1 Positive Effects of Demonetization

The surgical strike of the demonetization drive did help to eradicate black money but in a very limited way. People who were holding black money in cash were discouraged to a very limited extent from carrying out any transactions, for fear of getting caught by the tax and investigating authorities.

The Indian Government implemented this drive with an aim of going cashless so that more and more people and their cash are brought under the authority radar. Going cashless or digital is just in its initial, beginning phase and it will take a few years for it to fully realize.

Another advantage given by the Indian Government was that this drive will boost the banking sector as new legal money will enter the system. This drive hoped and anticipated that in the long run, interest rates on loans are expected to come down as higher tax revenues will be collected due to better tax compliance, and this in turn would help to reduce rates. However, it needs to be observed how much money actually remains in the banking system, once the cash withdrawal limits are lifted. This will lead to an increase in bank deposits and this may boost the credit creation system. But for this process to occur and sustain itself, banks (public sector units) that have bad loans need to be recapitalized, which in itself is a burden on the Indian Government.

Yet another benefit cited by the Indian government was that it is also hopeful that this move will reduce the cost and risk of handling cash. The government also estimated that approximately five lakh crore rupees may come back to it in the form of taxes and penalties. This in turn would help the government to deal with the fiscal deficit and to reduce its liability.

The Indian Government had also stated that this drive will minimize tax avoidance as whatever money will be exchanged or deposited, it will be carefully scrutinized. Bank accounts in which excess cash deposits will be made during the 50-day window would be scrutinized and also limits were already set and if in case the limits were crossed, immediate reporting of the same would be done to the Income Tax department. Dealings in this period in sectors like jewelry and real estate would be under the radar and those entering into loan transactions may also undergo tax scrutiny. Search and seizure activities of the IT Department would also rise to curb such malpractices.

Banks launched several payment solutions, digital wallets and merchant transaction apps (ICICI Pockets, SBI Buddy, HDFC PayZapp, etc.) to help customers and merchants get into tune with online, digital transactions. They also catered to the needs of semi-rural and rural populations. Efforts were made to integrate several digital portals and wallets with the payment needs of small merchants in order to cater to small value payment options. E-commerce digital wallets, portals and platforms did witness a surge in usage and the opening of new accounts, but not in a big way. Mobile wallets like Paytm did witness a soaring growth in the post-demonetization period. "Paytm Karo" became the *mantra,* as Paytm the nation's largest mobile wallet became an alternative for cash for many. FreeCharge and MobiKwik too were quick enough to cash in on the cash crunch by widening their base and offers. FreeCharge did campaign intensively through its new slogan initiative "Lo Do Khatam Karo (take, give and seal the deal) to demonstrate to people how easily payments can be transferred. According to a study titled: "Indian M-wallet Market," mobile payment transaction value in India is also likely to cross 2,000 trillion rupees by Finance Year 2021-22 from just over eight trillion rupees as of Financial Year 2015-16.

Besides plastic money, the government had also promoted smartphone-based transactions through the Unified Payments Interface (UPI) during this drive. It facilitates simplified operations whereby users can make and receive payments via smartphones with direct transfer of funds within bank accounts.

Many criminal activities like extortion, money laundering, property, drug trafficking, etc., engage in black money transactions, political violence, religiously motivated violence, terrorism and abduction. In such cases, demonetization will be effective to a certain extent as these activities are carried out using high denomination currency. But demonetization will only be able to deal with high denomination currency in Indian rupees; the activities are also funded by other high denomination currencies which are beyond the scope and reach of this drive.

Black money and counterfeit currency fuel inflation. The Indian Government stated that inflation will be contained through demonetization, especially agriculture, land and housing prices (unorganized sector and secondary sales), etc., where a considerable portion of all transactions involve the cash component in black money. Demonetization would prove to be a useful means to deal with this unaccounted cash component.

The dream of the Indian Government to implement a cashless economy will be possible only if it will focus on spreading financial and economic literacy, and awareness and knowledge of infrastructure and technology among the masses. Ongoing efforts and programs to educate the masses are a must or when cash returns to the system, many would stop doing cashless transactions. It is said that while cash usage will drop in the future, but until such a time, it will be around for many years to come. Despite several measures, including such demonetization drives to mop up black money, the dirty game of black money continues to take on menacing proportions.

3.3.2 Negative Effects of Demonetization

The sudden withdrawal of high denomination currency is unjustified as it resulted in hardship to 90 percent of the population to target 10 percent of evaders and hoarders. Several economists and experts cited that this drive was more based on political calculations. Although the move did make waves, it was not a total success.

According to income tax experts, the massive hunt for undeclared money launched across the country post demonetization has revealed that this was either converted into gold or routed through shell companies to make it legal and white. Holding unaccounted income in the form of gold, jewelry, etc., can easily be shown as family heirlooms or possessions. This means the big fish continued to float above in the ocean of black money despite efforts to catch them through the net of this demonetization drive.

In a latest report from the World Gold Council (it is the market development organization for the gold industry), it is stated that gold demand from India was what supported global gold demand in the first quarter of 2017. This magnitude goes to show that India's hunger for gold is never-ending and a large part of this hunger is satiated through investing black money in gold. Nearly 70 to 80 percent of the transactions related to jewelry involve black money.

In August 2017, the Reserve Bank of India had estimated that 99 percent of the high denomination banknotes cancelled in the previous year were either deposited or exchanged for new currency. This goes to show that the demonetization exercise was not a complete success; these statistics are a blow to the Indian Government's claims that the drive would be successful in wiping out large amounts of black money. The RBI report also stated that a complex network of money laundering was set up immediately after this drive, which was used by rich Indians to deposit large sums of previously undeclared money without exposing themselves to tax authorities. They also sold old currency to brokers at a discounted price and thereafter, these brokers sent low-income people to either exchange or deposit them at various banks. The black money hoarders also used their friends and relatives to put their previously undeclared money into the banks.

Printing new currency is a costly affair and usually the government will have to bear costs that are higher than the benefits and in such a case, there is no use of demonetization. 164.57 crore rupees of black money in the new currency notes was seized in a little over a month after this drive, which really puts a question mark on the drive's effectiveness.

Indians, instead of going to work or college, stood in lines at the banks and ATM centers. Many cottage industries had to shut down due to which several people lost their jobs too, as they could not report to work because of their incessant waiting in long snake lines. The demand for Mahatma Gandhi National Rural Employment Guarantee Scheme (MGNREGS main aim is to enhance the livelihood security of people in rural areas) rose in the months of December 2016 and January 2017.

As 90 percent of the Indian economy is based on cash, the cash crunch situation did hit the economy for two quarters minimum. This cash crunch led to a chaotic situation especially in banks and ATM centers. ATMs had to be reconfigured to take in the new notes because they were of different dimensions than the ones they were replacing, and this upgrade was not thought of and took much longer to bring into effect than anticipated. Despite the assurance given by the Indian Government to improve cash availability, several banks and ATMs across the country continued to dispense little or no cash. They faced this cash crunch for a long time. This decision of banning high denomination currency without making provisions for cash availability was not welcome by most people, especially rural and semi-urban areas. Small businesses and working class were also hit badly by this move.

Novel and sophisticated methods like derivative instruments were also used a lot immediately after the announcement of the 2016 demonetization drive. Such instruments in the form of promissory notes, participatory notes, etc., were used by the tax evaders and money hoarders to convert their illegal money holdings into white money. Though Securities and Exchange Board of India (SEBI is the regulator for the securities market in India) tried to tighten the regulations and norms, but still the black money players found their way out through other routes like transfers taking place outside the nation. Thereafter, in the early part of 2017, SEBI announced that it would implement strict norms and reforms whereby SEBI decided to bar resident as well as non-resident Indians (NRIs) from making investments through participatory notes.

Property deals where black money dealings are rampant were not so much affected by this move. Rather several reports indicated otherwise, that this drive encouraged the corrupt bureaucrats and babus to ask for bribes and kickbacks in other forms like gold and new currency; they continued to mint money.

This drive caused great inconvenience to the common man, who was seen running from pillar to post or should we say from bank to bank and ATM to ATM. Another problem faced by the common man was in dealing with card-based transactions as he is not that well-versed with such dynamics.

It was disheartening to see people including elderly and women waiting patiently in the queues often for hours on end, for days on end, to get their notes exchanged. And this waiting went on for days together as there was a major cash crunch. This cash crunch hit the class of daily wage earners the hardest. As most villagers are reliant on hard cash notes for their livelihood, due to this drive, they were not even able to cover their day-to-day needs. Wholesale market dealers and small traders were also adversely affected.

The banking structure, especially in rural areas, is not that sound. This shaky structure was not able to handle such a huge transition, and moreover the time window of 50 days added more woes.

This drive also aimed at curbing counterfeit money used for financing terrorist activities, but this aim is a short-sighted one as terrorist activities are not merely financed by the Indian rupee. The American dollar and several other currencies are also used for these terrorism networks. Therefore, by merely banning counterfeit Indian currency, curbing the terrorism network won't be possible.

It was also reported that old cash was dumped or burnt in bulk in several locations across the nation. These cash dumps should have reached the Indian Government, but that did not happen; hence the purpose of this drive was not met 100 percent.

A Word of Caution

Demonetization will not get back the money concealed away in offshore havens and foreign banks. Demonetization only helps to convert the black money into white in a limited manner, thereby adding it to the government treasury and minimizing future plundering of money. But the money that has already been stashed away needs to be recovered by techniques other than banning high denomination currency.

The poor class and the middle class have always lost their household savings to various schemes by the Indian Government, and this demonetization drive is no exception. The sad part of this is that these household savings are a result of hard-earned money. As usual due to diminishing household savings, honest and hardworking people are forced to save less and spend more on goods. The more the people spend on goods, the higher will be the economic growth rate and GDP. All this at whose cost—of course at the cost of the poor class and middle class. And who gets away as usual—the rich and the elite.

Spotlight

All deaths or suicides have been of people belonging to the poor and middle class families; these classes were put into dire circumstances due to the cash crunch caused by the ban. There were no deaths or suicides in the real hard-core black money hoarders' community. Even during the demonetization drive and in the post-demonetization period, they were having grand parties and lavish weddings, and there were bundles and bundles of new currency floating in the mansions of the rich, while the *aam aadmi* (the common man) continued and still continues to struggle to make both ends meet...old or new currency—does not matter.

The Indian Government received a lot of flak from the people for its erratic string of rule changes over the period of 50 days of demonetization. It is evident that demonetization has both pros and cons, and it is up to the Indian Government to weigh all the pros and cons and then decide whether it is beneficial to go ahead with such demonetization drives (or not) in the future.

3.3.3 Post-Demonetization

When the demonetization drive was announced by the Indian Government in November 2016, it stated two main reasons for doing this: elimination of counterfeit currency and destabilization of the black money market.

> **A Word of Caution**
>
> This policy move was short-sighted as it targeted only a negligible percentage of the black money hoarders. Even if the government believed that this drive would be able to suck out all the black cash in circulation, the activities that generated such money still continued in the aftermath.

Demonetization is no silver bullet against the fake currency or black money problem. If old notes can be counterfeited so can new ones. Counterfeit notes of 500 rupee denomination have increased by 46 percent and 1000 rupee denomination by over 100 percent in the last five years. All means and provisions of printing fake money need to be eliminated; this is what needs to be done first before implementing any such drive in the future. According to IndiaSpend (IndiaSpend is India's first data journalism initiative) analysis of government data, in the period 2015-16, only 16 of every 250 fake notes in India were detected. According to RBI statistics, of the 90.26 billion Indian currency notes in circulation in the period 2015-16, no more than 0.63 million or seven in a million were detected as counterfeit.

Table 6: Counterfeit Currency Detected During the Period 2015-16

Denomination	Counterfeit Notes	Notes in Circulation (million)	Counterfeit (%)	Counterfeit Value (₹)	Total Value (₹)
2, 5	2	11,626	0	7	4,069.1 crore
10	134	32,015	0	1,340	32,015 crore
20	96	4,924	0	1,920	9,848 crore

Denomination	Counterfeit Notes	Notes in Circulation (million)	Counterfeit (%)	Counterfeit Value (₹)	Total Value (₹)
50	6453	3,890	0.0000017	322,650	19,450 crore
100	221447	15,778	0.000014	2.21 crore	1,57,780 crore
500	261695	15,707	0.0000167	13.09 crore	7,85,350 crore
100	143099	6,326	0.0000226	14.31 crore	6,32,600 crore

Source: Reserve Bank of India Data

The other side of the anti-black money drive is online and cashless economy. This side too is myopic in its approach. The volume of electronic money transactions dropped in the post-demonetization period. The value of transactions now is closer to the value in November 2016 at ₹ 94 trillion, when this demonetization drive began. Except for Unified Payments Interface, all other electronic payment options saw a dip in both transaction volumes and value. Most small business owners do not have technology infrastructure like card readers; hence the cashless economy that the Indian Government is envisioning won't become a reality overnight. According to the Pew Research Centre (a non-partisan American "fact tank," which provides analysis and research information about the attitudes, issues and trends shaping America and the world), only 22 percent of adults in India have access to the Internet. This shows that the vast majority of the Indian population who do not have access to the Internet will be unable to use online banking and its features. According to the Reserve Bank of India, as of 2016, the average number of card transactions per inhabitant is amongst the lowest in the world at 6.7. We are talking of 1.2+ billion people with a huge percent lacking even access to basic necessities. Moreover, certain segments of the population like senior citizens will find it extremely difficult to switch from hard cash to digital transactions. The report "Economic and Social Survey of Asia and Pacific 2017" published by the United Nations pointed out the gaps in India's digital drive, "Moving towards a cashless economy will require addressing household determinants of cash dependence beyond technology adoption, including low financial inclusion, high informality, persistent gender inequality in access to finance, low financial literacy, low

ICT infrastructure and large gaps in energy access." All these statistics show that Indians prefer cash to cashless transactions.

Moreover, this myopic measure hit the lower segment of the Indian society really hard, as people from this segment depend heavily on daily wages in cash for their livelihoods. Even small and medium businesses suffered as they too need hard cash for meeting their requirements like paying wages and procuring raw materials. Pulling out all the cash from the economy is synonymous to draining out all the blood from a person's body. Just as such a person would collapse, a similar situation occurred after the demonetization drive. This situation caused immense trouble to small traders, daily wage earners, farmers, households, etc., who were not able to get their salaries and due to a lack of cash, they were not able to afford basic necessities like food, healthcare and shelter. This also led to a lot of unemployment of the innocent and several suicide cases also occurred. Demonetization reportedly claimed 45+ deaths within eight days of its launch. In the jewelry sector, 15-20 percent of the labor force and in the leather industry, 20-25 percent of the labor force had been adversely affected. Overall, the employment aspect of the informal, unorganized sector was severely hit. The agriculture sector was also adversely affected as farmers suffered heavy losses and had to sale their produce at throw away prices due to cash shortage and lack of demand on account of unemployment. Several vegetables like potatoes and onions had to be thrown away and this resulted in huge wastage of valuable produce. All these factors affected the growth of this sector.

The 2016 demonetization drive of moving away from cash to the cashless, digitized transactions was meant to encourage financial investments like bank deposits, shares, etc., and to discourage transactions related to sectors like real estate, gold, etc., where a major pie of black money is present. But real-time statistics and results showed an opposite picture. If cashless transactions could curtail black money then Kenya would have been the most transparent nation in the world as it is running on almost a cashless economy. But this is not the case; Kenya was listed as one of the world's most corrupt nations in Transparency

International's 2015 Corruption Perception Index. Therefore, a digital economy is not the silver bullet for the menace of black money.

The huge distress that the demonetization of 2016 caused makes it impossible for any future governments to introduce any stringent measures to curb the hoarding and circulation of black money. The note ban blues really did not affect the corrupt elite and blue blood class. Meanwhile, black money transactions, scams and illegal activities have continued to grow after a brief hiatus. In conclusion, the demonetization scheme or any of the support measures like promoting credit card use, linking biometric identities to bank accounts, etc., will not solve the problem of the black economy permanently. In conclusion, despite this demonetization drive, the total amount of black money that had been destabilized was significantly small. The demonetization drive was able to only destabilize a small segment of the black money economy, but the main sufferer was and still continues to be the common man.

3.4 EFFECTS OF GOODS AND SERVICES TAX ON BLACK MONEY

The Indian Government introduced the Goods and Services Tax (GST is an indirect tax that will be levied on every value addition) in July 2017 with an aim to expand the tax net and introduce a simplified, seamless, uniform tax system. The main goal of GST is to replace the layers of various taxes (service, surcharge, advertisement, VAT and excise) with an aim of doing away with the cascading effects of taxes by unifying taxes under one tax structure. Over 1200 items have been put in four broad tax categories. The government said that this new tax rollout will bring about a new governance culture, simplify tax structure and will help to prevent black money.

Under the GST guidelines, all the purchases and sales invoices are required to be uploaded on the online website Goods and Services Tax Identification Number (GSTIN) every month as a part of tracking all components of the supply chain. In case a seller or trader gives out a false bill or does not show the exact amount received, the buyer of the goods will be intimated about the same through the GSTIN. Also the buyer will be denied the credit of the goods. These checks will make the buyer avoid such sellers/traders. Such transaction anomalies are automatically reported to the government. The system of GSTIN will help to identify any untraceable transactions with the help of in-built intelligence tools and checks. No trader or seller will be able sell goods without proper bills.

Permanent account number and Aadhaar card number will be required to file GST returns. Under the GST migration plan, every PAN holder will be assigned a temporary registration number, called the Goods and Services Tax Identification Number (GSTIN). A login ID and password is also provided to access the GST online portal so that people can provide all their details and supporting documents. Thereafter, the assessee will be assigned an Application Reference Number (ARN) after submitting enrollment application, which will help existing taxpayers to migrate into the new tax regime portal.

Spotlight

There would be a rating system also, through which sellers and traders would be rated. In case of defaulters, the sellers or traders will get a bad rating. Potential buyers would not buy from sellers and traders with bad ratings. This data will also be shared with the Income tax department. All these techniques and tools will make it difficult for the sellers and traders to carry out their black money deals.

Essentially speaking, it is hoped by the Indian Government that by digitizing all transaction-related components of the entire supply chain process, the main one being bills/invoices, the magnitude of black money can be considerably reduced. Also the dual monitoring mechanism of all things related to GST by the Central and State Governments will help to improve the tax regime and its related functions; hence improve the tax compliance and eventually curtail the black economy.

With the above advantages of GST, comes a plethora of disadvantages that are more than likely to dilute the advantages. After the GST rollout, India faced nationwide protests, strikes and downed shutters, and this disrupted business. Farmers, traders, and small and medium-sized enterprises had planned a series of protests through July and August 2017. The unorganized sector too registered its protest. The Bhartiya Udyog Vyapar Mandal (BUVM is a pan-India organization that aims to improve the welfare and economic progress of the business community and eventually the nation) had called for a strike on 30 June 2017 and had sent letters to all associations across India seeking support to raise objections against certain provisions in GST. This clearly indicated that there was a mixed reaction of protest and support towards this new tax reform. New or small-time traders are not tech-savvy and do not have much knowledge of the online world; hence they will need to hire professional assistance and services to get them onto the GST digital route. But such professional services are costly and this adds burden to their operating costs. Most small and medium-sized enterprises are not much aware of the dynamics and the finer nuances of GST. ClearTax GST software can help to solve some of these issues. This software provides a simplified solution for filing GST returns and generating GST invoices, and it also provides hands-on training. Most established business have their own Enterprise Resource Planning software in place for handling tax returns, service tax, VAT, etc., but with the introduction of GST, they will need to either upgrade their existing software or purchase the new GST-compliant software. Buying the new software will add burden to their operating cost as well as training cost. Companies are required to register for GST in each state that they operate in; this multiple state registration is a cumbersome process. As the GST system has gone live during the middle of a financial year, companies and businesses will end up following both the old and new tax systems in parallel. And this has resulted in compliance issues. Certain retail products had only four percent tax on them. After GST, such products could become or rather have become more expensive for the consumers. GST may be a boon for enterprises, service providers, manufacturers and sellers, but not in the case of consumers. Being an indirect tax, GST will ultimately create quite a large hole in the pockets of the end consumers.

Several months into the GST reform, it is evident that the consumers and the common man are the main sufferers as they have to bear higher indirect costs, and not the black money hoarders. When Australia introduced GST in 2000, the Australian Government had created a commission to safeguard the interests of consumers. This commission kept a tab on the prices to ensure that consumers received full benefits from the reduction in tax rates. If the tax rates went up, it was ensured that consumers were not charged more than what was necessary. Given the unstable political climate in India, it is unlikely for India to follow in Australia's footsteps. Change is definitely never easy. Right after the implementation of demonetization and then the GST rollout, India's economy will take at least 1 to 2 years to become stable. Ideally speaking, the Indian Government should have started with low rates, achieved compliance and confidence of the public, and then should have gradually pushed the rates up.

3.5 CHAPTER RECAP

1. Politicians and businessmen swindle huge funds from banks. Moreover, several of these bank funds and loans are diverted for other purposes than the official purposes for which they have been granted.

2. Modern-day banking needs technology to process its transactions. During the 2016 demonetization drive, banks should have played a more proactive and intensive role in using technology tools to nab the black marketers and tax evaders. In certain cases, the exact opposite scenario was witnessed; officials of some of the private sector banks were alleged to have helped those with black money to launder funds during the demonetization drive.

3. According to statistics by the Global Financial Integrity (GFI), counterfeit money deposited into non-Indian banks by the Indian politicians, businessmen and celebrities since 1991 pegs at a whopping 2,100,000 crore rupees.

4. Switzerland has recently given a green signal for automatic exchange of financial account information (AEI) with India.

India will be able to access all the transactions between Indians and Swiss banks from 2019 onwards, but this 'delay' time window will give black money account holders plenty of time to move their illegal money to other tax havens in order to avoid their information being shared with the Indian Government.

5. By just recovering a few million dollars of stashed away cash, we cannot expect to see the Indian horizon cleared off of the air of black money; hoarders, fraudsters and defaulters need to be brought to book immediately.

6. As per the estimates revealed by the Swiss National Bank, the total amount of money held in Swiss banks by foreign clients from across the world increased from 1.41 trillion Swiss francs to 1.42 trillion Swiss francs during 2016. India was ranked 61 in 2015 and 75 in 2016. India was ranked highest at position 37 in the year 2004.

7. In 2014, as much as three-fifths of India's total gold imports came from Switzerland; India imported 471.9 tons of gold from Switzerland. This was done by over-invoicing the gold imports from Switzerland, which helped them to bring back the black money as white money into the nation.

8. Income Tax department, Enforcement Directorate and Central Bureau of Investigation should conduct regular searches of various banks across India to keep a tab on their functioning and to spot if there are any suspicious transactions.

9. Many landowners do not grow crops on their land; they use their land for different purposes. However, after the demonetization of 2016, they showed the source of their incomes as the sale of produce/crops at a higher price. However, these transactions existed only in books. In this way, these landowners managed to deposit their black money without coming under the lens of scrutiny. The banks, too, did not bother to verify such claims.

10. The unaccounted money held in foreign bank accounts generated through hawala deals needs to be put under strict investigation and under the lens of the national and international investigating agencies.

11. Withdrawing of high denomination currency notes has been done before in 1946 and in 1978, and now in the recent past it was initiated in November 2016. The Indian Government undertook demonetization on November 8, 2016. Social media and news channels have been filled with public frenzy, stories and reactions in relation to this currency purge right from day one since its announcement.

12. The surgical strike of the demonetization drive did help to eradicate black money but in a very limited way. People who were holding black money in cash were discouraged to a very limited extent from carrying out any transactions, for fear of getting caught by the tax and investigating authorities.

13. Another advantage given by the Indian Government was that this drive will boost the banking sector as new legal money will enter the system. This drive hoped and anticipated that in the long run, interest rates on loans are expected to come down as higher tax revenues will be collected due to better tax compliance, and this in turn would help to reduce rates. However, it needs to be observed how much money actually remains in the banking system, once the cash withdrawal limits are lifted.

14. The Indian Government had also stated that this drive will minimize tax avoidance as whatever money will be exchanged or deposited, it will be carefully scrutinized. Bank accounts in which excess cash deposits will be made during the 50-day window would be scrutinized and also limits were already set and if in case the limits were crossed, immediate reporting of the same would be done to the Income Tax department.

15. Banks launched several payment solutions, digital wallets and merchant transaction apps (ICICI Pockets, SBI Buddy, HDFC PayZapp, etc.) to help customers and merchants get into tune with online, digital transactions. They also catered to the needs of semi-rural and rural populations.

16. The dream of the Indian Government to implement a cashless economy will be possible only if it will focus on spreading financial and economic literacy, and awareness and knowledge of infrastructure and technology among the masses.

Ongoing efforts and programs to educate the masses are a must or when cash returns to the system, many would stop doing cashless transactions.

17. The sudden withdrawal of high denomination currency is unjustified as it resulted in hardship to 90 percent of the population to target 10 percent of evaders and hoarders. Several economists and experts cited that this drive was more based on political calculations. Although the move did make waves, it was not a total success.

18. Printing new currency is a costly affair and usually the government will have to bear costs that are higher than the benefits and in such a case, there is no use of demonetization. 164.57 crore rupees of black money in the new currency notes was seized in a little over a month after this drive, which really puts a question mark on the drive's effectiveness.

19. Indians, instead of going to work or college, stood in lines at the banks and ATM centers. Many cottage industries had to shut down due to which several people lost their jobs too, as they could not report to work because of their incessant waiting in long snake lines.

20. As 90 percent of the Indian economy is based on cash, the cash crunch situation did hit the economy for two quarters minimum. This cash crunch led to a chaotic situation especially in banks and ATM centers. ATMs had to be reconfigured to take in the new notes because they were of different dimensions than the ones they were replacing, and this upgrade was not thought of and took much longer to bring into effect than anticipated.

21. This drive caused great inconvenience to the common man, who was seen running from pillar to post or should we say from bank to bank and ATM to ATM. Another problem faced by the common man was in dealing with card-based transactions as he is not that well-versed with such dynamics.

22. This cash crunch hit the class of daily wage earners the hardest. As most villagers are reliant on hard cash notes for their livelihood, due to this drive, they were not even able to cover their day-to-day needs. Wholesale market dealers and small traders were also adversely affected.

23. This drive also aimed at curbing counterfeit money used for financing terrorist activities, but this aim is a short-sighted one as terrorist activities are not merely financed by the Indian rupee. The American dollar and several other currencies are also used for these terrorism networks. Therefore, by merely banning counterfeit Indian currency, curbing the terrorism network won't be possible.

24. The poor class and the middle class have always lost their household savings to various schemes by the Indian government, and this demonetization drive is no exception.

25. Demonetization reportedly claimed 45+ deaths within eight days of its launch. In the jewelry sector, 15-20 percent of the labor force and in the leather industry, 20-25 percent of the labor force had been adversely affected. Overall, the employment aspect of the informal, unorganized sector was severely hit. The agriculture sector was also adversely affected as farmers suffered heavy losses and had to sale their produce at throw away prices due to cash shortage and lack of demand on account of unemployment.

26. The demonetization drive was able to only destabilize a small segment of the black money economy, but the main sufferer was and still continues to be the common man.

27. The Indian Government introduced the Goods and Services Tax (GST is an indirect tax that will be levied on every value addition) in July 2017 with an aim to expand the tax net and introduce a simplified, seamless, uniform tax system.

28. Under the GST guidelines, all the purchases and sales invoices are required to be uploaded on the online website Goods and Services Tax Identification Number (GSTIN) every month as a part of tracking all components of the supply chain.

29. There would be a rating system also, through which sellers and traders would be rated. In case of defaulters, the sellers or traders will get a bad rating. Potential buyers would not buy from sellers and traders with bad ratings.

30. After the GST rollout, India faced nationwide protests, strikes and downed shutters, and this disrupted business. Farmers, traders, and small and medium-sized enterprises had

planned a series of protests through July and August 2017. The unorganized sector too registered its protest. The Bhartiya Udyog Vyapar Mandal (BUVM is a pan-India organization that aims to improve the welfare and economic progress of the business community and eventually the nation) had called for a strike on 30 June 2017 and had sent letters to all associations across India seeking support to raise objections against certain provisions in GST. This clearly indicated that there was a mixed reaction of protest and support towards this new tax reform.

31. New or small-time traders are not tech-savvy and do not have much knowledge of the online world; hence they will need to hire professional assistance and services to get them onto the GST digital route. But such professional services are costly and this adds burden to their operating costs.

32. Companies are required to register for GST in each state that they operate in; this multiple state registration is a cumbersome process. As the GST system has gone live during the middle of a financial year, companies and businesses will end up following both the old and new tax systems in parallel. And this has resulted in compliance issues.

33. GST may be a boon for enterprises, service providers, manufacturers and sellers, but not in the case of consumers. Being an indirect tax, GST will ultimately create quite a large hole in the pockets of the end consumers.

34. Several months into the GST reform, it is evident that the consumers and the common man are the main sufferers as they have to bear higher indirect costs, and not the black money hoarders.

3.6 QUESTIONS FOR REFLECTION

1. How black money is detrimental to the economic health of India?
2. What about black money invested in property and gold?
3. Why is it that only the common man suffers and the powerful get away?

4. Why have wealthy individuals become more cautious while investing their black money in foreign banks?
5. What is demonetization and does it really serve the purpose of curbing black money?
6. Was the demonetization drive of 2016 a plan designed to convert black money into white?
7. Will GST help in curbing black money?
8. Can the effects of demonetization and GST be quantified?

Chapter 4

More Black Money Dynamics

The evil of black money does not revolve around a particular nation, but it is a global phenomenon. Black money or *Kala Dhan* has elicited widespread debate in recent times, and this has led to a renewed interest of both Indian and global scholars and academic communities who are constantly studying the various conundrums related to black money. Money is present in two forms: visible and hidden. Visible is something that all can see and can be taxed whereas the hidden form is concealed, illegal and can easily escape from the net of taxation, and this is where the real problem lies.

In 2014, India's GDP was approximate 2.047 trillion dollars. The government was expecting to collect taxes and duties amounting to 13.64 lakh crore rupees. This means that there was another 75 percent of this, about 10.4 lakh crore rupees, which it missed out on because it was involved in the black money transactions.

There is a whopping sum of 4,479 crore rupees in bank accounts abroad that has not been accounted for and that is only one small slice of the big black money pie that is stashed away in Hong Kong and Shanghai Banking Corporation's Geneva branch.

Tax havens have always been a subject of discussion, but recently they have been the centre of attraction in the international circuit. In the last three decades, they have become a global business in themselves by offering low tax rates thereby domestic tax evasion and money laundering through strict financial secrecy laws has increased a lot.

No matter which measure the Indian Government and investigating agencies implement to bring about a decline in unaccounted cash or black money, the players of this dirty game continue to find clever ways to continue this game. These dynamics make this game all the more unpredictable. They use the grey areas of legislations and laws and the informal sector to continue with the generation of black money. For example, in the period after the demonetization drive of 2016 was announced, the black money dynamics saw a surge in the demand for informal chit funds, which operate purely on the basis of trust and reliability. Due to their ability to absorb black money while maintaining secrecy and anonymity, and also ensuring that there is no transaction trail, informal chit funds were and are still used as safe spots by individuals and businesses to park their money. During the post-demonetization period, chit fund operators were quick enough to capitalize on this opportunity by increasing the number of chit groups or increasing the size of the chit installment. Such black money dynamics prove that no measure or drive can stop the black economy from continuing to operate as there are numerous methods by which it can be generated, which may or may not depend on cash circulation.

4.1 EFFECTS OF BLACK MONEY IN INDIA

The magnitude and evilness of black money in India can be measured through its effects. The ever-expanding magnitude of black money still continues to haunt the Indian landscape till this very day.

1. Vicious Cycle of Black Money and Corruption—Black money and corruption go hand-in-hand. Since most black money transactions are done through illegal means, they add to the corruption levels.

2. Misuse of Resources—The floating of black money in the economy facilitates the misuse of resources for negative means. This misuse of resources also leads to the rise of anti-social elements in the society. People with more money, especially black money, think that they can use their monetary power to monopolize and establish their sole right on all resources and sectors.

3. **Inflation and Increased Taxes**—As the people who have evaded tax have more money at their disposal, they are ready to spend more than what is necessary to get what they want, whereas the common man is caught in a loop of paying his dues on the one hand and not being able to keep up with the rise in prices on the other hand. It is but natural that if the black money is brought back to the Indian Government's treasury, the government will have more money in its hands and thereby the tax burden on the people can be reduced. Black money limits or dilutes the Reserve Bank of India policies that are formed to target inflation.

4. **Adulterated or Counterfeit Goods**—In a number of developing nations, critical and life-saving medicines are in short supply and they are often procured through the black market as there are no other alternatives available. Such a situation is dangerous, especially in the case of adulterated or substandard medicines, as they can prove to be fatal for the patients consuming them.

5. **Loss of Tax Revenue to the National Exchequer**—Black money is about tax avoidance and evasion, and this causes a great loss of revenue to the national exchequer. This loss translates to low level of social growth and economic progress. As the government is not able to receive the required level of monetary funds, it is unable to spend on the much-needed welfare schemes or infrastructure facilities. This loss of revenue also leads to an increase in the Indian Government's deficit. In order to balance this deficit, the government has to increase taxes and decrease subsidies. It also needs to borrow funds and this borrowing leads to more debt.

6. **False Estimates**—The menace of black money has such a deep magnitude that it skews the estimates of various economic factors like GDP, per capita income, etc. The skewed statistics do not give the correct status of the health of the economy and

nation. Such skewed statistics lead to fault policy planning and ineffective measures.

4.2 INDIAN STATISTICS

A variety of methods are used for deriving the magnitude, estimates and statistics of black money, both in India and on a global level, but each source results in the generation of divergent estimates and statistics. There are several methods like circulation velocity method, input-output ratio method, and sampling method to arrive at black money estimates.

> **A Word of Caution**
>
> All these estimation methods involve a lot of assumptions and adjustments; hence the estimates cannot be accurate but only indicative. The Indian Government also does not have accurate figures; even the government does not know how much of the money is related to tax evasion alone and how much is derived from criminal activities.

'Who all have black money?' and 'How much do they have?' are two major questions that crop up in the mind of every single *aam aadmi* (common man) of India. Although there is no single solid hard evidence, yet here are some estimates and figures of the magnitude of black money in India. According to the Government of India (2012), the extent of black money is somewhere between $500 billion and $1400 billion. Other estimates include an average of ₹ 1,36,466 crore or $27.3 billion stashed annually during 2002 to 2006; which means about ₹ 6,92,328 crore or $136.5 billion hoarded in the five-year period (Global Financial Integrity Report, 2006), ₹ 9,295 crore stashed in Swiss banks by Indians (White Paper, Government of India), a World Bank report puts India's shadow economy at close to one-fifth of the economic output, and many more such shocking statistics are shared in various national and international reports, books, surveys and findings.

As per the Indian Income Tax department, based on the tax returns of the financial years 2013, 2014 and 2015, the following are some of the main sectors that contribute to the black money economy of the nation: manufacturing, trading, real estate and services. According to the Report on Illicit Financial Flows by Global Financial Integrity, approximately 510 billion dollars of black money flowed out of India in the period from 2004 to 2013, which was more than the foreign direct investment (FDI) received. The outflow peaked in 2012 when it reached 92.9 billion dollars. Illicit Financial Flows or IFFs are defined as movements of money or capital from one country to another that is illegally earned, transferred, or utilized (http://www.gfintegrity.org/issue/illicit-fnancial-fows/).

Table 7: Illicit Financial Outflows from India, 2004-13

Year	Amount (in billion dollars)
2004	19.5
2005	20.3
2006	27.8
2007	34.5
2008	47.2
2009	29.2
2010	70.3
2011	85.6
2012	92.9
2013	83
Total	**510.3**

Tax havens play a crucial role in the generation of illicit financial flows. As tax havens provide opportunities to wealthy individuals and corporations to evade taxes, escape tax scrutiny, secrecy and anonymity provisions, and have very low tax rates, makes them profitable locations for illicit financial flows.

According to Global Financial Integrity (GFI), India lost 123 billion dollars in black money during the period from 2001 to 2010. The National Institute of Public Finance and Policy (NIPFP is a premier research institution in public economics and policies under India's Ministry of Finance) estimated that in 1985 the amount of black money in India was nearly 1,00,000 crore rupees and it was approximately 20 percent of the national income. Fast forward 10 years, this amount figure was believed to be more than 4,00,000 crore rupees. Compare these recent figures with old estimates and the difference is shocking.

Nicholas Kaldor, a Cambridge economist, in his report on India Tax Reform assessed black income estimates to the tune of 600 crores rupees in 1953-54, which was 6 percent of Gross National Product. Wanchoo Committee estimated the amount of black income at 700 crore rupees in 1961-62, which was 4.4 percent of Gross National Product and then at 1,000 crore rupees and 1,400 crore rupees in 1965-66 and 1968-69 respectively. Apart from the above official estimates, several unofficial estimates of black money also are carried out and discussed in the academic communities. Whether official or unofficial, all these estimates reveal one common factor: 90 percent of the money and wealth is owned by the 10 percent of the population.

India is in the top five for under-reporting in exports—India ranks number five on the list of "Twenty Largest Export Under-Invoicers with Respective Export Proceeds Requirements". To explain in layman's terms: an Indian business man sells his goods abroad each worth rupees 10 and claims his products are for only seven rupees on the invoice in order to pay lesser taxes and duties. Here the difference of 3 Rupees = Black Money.

According to the Interpol estimates, the size of hawala done by Indian operators is pegged at possibly 40 percent of the nation's Gross Domestic Product. In India, hawala is considered a civil offence and people violating its provisions are penalized with a fine up to three times the amount detected in an infringement.

Table 8: Black Money of Indians in Swiss Bank
(In Crore ₹)

Year	Black Money
2006	41,400
2007	27,500
2008	15,400
2009	12,600
2010	12,450
2011	14,000
2012	9,000
2013	14,000

India Human Development Surveys have shown an increase in income inequality over the years. Some statistics report about 419 billion dollars in taxable income and profits being laundered out of the nation over the past decade. The National Sample Survey consumption surveys have shown an increase in consumption inequality over the years. And the common culprit is black money.

In the wake of the recent demonetization drive of 2016, the following figures have come to light: the searches conducted by the Income Tax Department between April 2014 and November 2016 on 1356 groups of assessees led to admission of undisclosed income of 31,277 crore rupees apart from seizure of undisclosed assets worth 2,164 crore rupees.

Before the Panama Papers leak occurred, according to the Indian Government estimates, an estimated one trillion dollars of Indian black money was believed to be stashed away in offshore locations. In the last 40+ years, India has lost at least 17 trillion rupees to tax havens. India has exported goods and services worth at least 17 trillion rupees over the past four decades but did not remit an equivalent amount in foreign exchange. This analysis was provided by the *Hindustan Times* (HT is an Indian English language daily newspaper) based on the Reserve Bank of India (RBI) data gleaned from the period from 1972 to 2015. The RBI data is based on 1,88,605 export transactions that were not remitted home, and apart from phony export deals, Indians resorted to over-invoicing of imports and under-invoicing of exports. Over-invoicing of imports and under-invoicing of exports are the two main ways through which black money hoarders and operators can transfer their funds abroad. According to the 1988 study by the Central Economic Intelligence Bureau (CEIB is an Indian intelligence agency), an estimated 13,000 crore rupees of exports were not remitted to India. Some of the amount was recovered but according to the latest RBI data statistics, realization of more than ₹ 3,200 crore from that period is still pending.

Black money is accumulated through different sources. The three main sources of black money are corruption, hawala and crime. Among these sources, corruption is the chief villain.

4.2.1 Key Scams and Scandals of Corruption and Black Money in India

I am sharing some reference material from my own book: *Corruption in India: Causes, Effects and Reforms*. Black money and corruption scams, swindles or scandals—all mean one thing—disgrace to a nation. The following list is but a mere drop of the deep ocean of black money and corruption in India; the cauldron of black money and corruption is constantly boiling to the brim with scams. If we were to detail out each and every scam, it would take several volumes to do so. Undoubtedly, there is one common factor running through the long list of scams—the truth, which the sincere taxpayer has every right to know but it never ever reaches him; they both are the biggest victim.

Let us take a quick scan of some of the major scams that occurred on the Indian horizon from 1948 till recent times. The ultimate aim of all these scandals is the accumulation of black money in offshore bank accounts and tax havens.

1. **Jeep Purchase (1948)**—by distorting regulations and bypassing protocols, a deal worth 80 lakh rupees for jeeps for the Indian Army in Kashmir was signed with a foreign firm. The case for this scam was closed in 1955, despite the demand of the opposition for judicial inquiry.
2. **Mundhra Scandal (1957)**—the first big financial scandal of free India in the 1950s. It involved the sale of fictitious shares to the insurance giant, Life Insurance Corporation. The investment was done under governmental pressure and in the process LIC lost most of the money.
3. **Bofors Payoff (1987)**—a major scandal of the 1980s. Here several prominent politicians, high profile businessmen and brokers were accused of receiving massive kickbacks from Bofors AB for winning a bid to supply India's 155 mm field howitzer. A well-thought out cover-up operation was mounted by the accused in order to displace the inquiry into the allegations

of commission payments. Most of the accused have died of old age whereas the investigation is still going on. The sheer mismanagement of public resources involved in this scam is shocking as the amount of money spent on the investigation is much higher than the amount involved in alleged kickbacks, payoffs and commission payments. For more than two decades, this scam has been in the news circuit.

4. **Securities scam** (1992)—it involved misappropriation of funds to the tune of over ₹ 3500 crore. The stock market and money market were in doldrums, and there was a prolonged closure of the stock exchanges. There was deep panic among brokers and investors. The share market faced a massive loss to the tune of ₹ 100,000 crore.
5. And many more....

India was hit by a series of scams since independence, but in the year 2010, India had been rocked by a series of big scandals. India is known for its traditions and cultural heritage, but the recent series of scams involving unimaginably large amounts of money has tarnished its image on the international front. The scams in India have increased in scope, scale and audacity over the years, in a rapid manner. According to research figures, the total amount of money involved in various scams over the last 10-15 years is estimated to be over a mind-boggling ₹ 80 trillion. In the last 10-15 years, some of the top corruption scams that have grabbed headlines and exposed high profile people are as follows:

1. **Hawala Scam** (1996)—Hawala is the biggest ever scandal in the world which involved over 115 top politicians and bureaucrats of the country. It involved the alleged payments that politicians received from hawala brokers. Due to the lack of hard evidence, everyone was let off. Hawala is a system of underground banking purely based on trust whereby money can be made available internationally without actually moving it or leaving a record of transactions.

2. **Fodder Scam** (1996)—a corruption scandal that involved the alleged embezzlement of about 950 crore from the state government treasury of the eastern Indian state of Bihar. Ministers, corporates and bureaucrats colluded to bill the state treasury over ₹ 950 crore to provide medicines, animal husbandry equipment and feed for "vast herds of fictitious livestock".
3. **Tehelka Sting** (2001)—through its sting operation 'Operation Westend,' Tehelka exposed the corruption underlying India's large defense contracts. This operation was a major milestone in investigative journalism.
4. **Scorpene Submarine Deal** (2005)—secret Navy documents were sold to the makers of the Scorpene submarine, Thales, through various middlemen from the Navy. 500 crore rupees were alleged to have been paid to government decision-makers by Thales.
5. **Stamp Paper Scam** (2006)—this multi-crore scam involved complex and expansive counterfeiting of stamp paper, and it had spread its web of operations across 12 states. It involved selling of fake stamp papers to bulk purchasers like insurance companies, stock market players and banks. The scam involved the sale of not only counterfeit stamp paper but also related items such as revenue stamps, foreign bills, judicial court fee stamps, broker notes, etc.
6. **Satyam Computers Scam** (2009)—the biggest fraud in the Indian corporate world involving approximately 70 billion Indian rupees. In this scam, the company's financial records had been fudged and manipulated and profit levels were falsely inflated for the last several years. Approximately 1.5 billion US dollars of the company's past funds were "non-existent". It is dubbed as "India's Enron".
7. **2G Spectrum** (2010)—by far the biggest political scam in modern Indian history. Here the telecom bandwidth was being grossly undervalued and offered

to a chosen few with vested interests, resulting in a huge loss amounting to a humongous figure of 40 billion dollars. Dubious 2G licenses were distributed at throw-away prices that were pegged at 2001 prices. The groups involved in this scam—politicians and bureaucrats who had the authority to sell the licenses, media professional who liaised between the politicians and corporations, and corporations who were buying the frequency allocation licenses.

8. **Commonwealth Games** (2010)—right from the infrastructure projects to medical equipment, everything was overrated, and there were huge misappropriations, over-inflated prices and discrepancies in tenders. The whole project was shrouded in a blanket of allegations—right from environmental concerns to racism. This ₹ 8000 crore scam was unearthed by the Comptroller and Auditor General of India even before the conduct of the games. The Central Bureau of Investigation and India's anti-corruption watchdog have identified more than 16 projects with possible irregularities.
9. **Adarsh Housing Society** (2010)—the Adarsh Society is a cooperative society in the city of Mumbai; it was reserved for the war widows and veterans of the Kargil War. Right from plot procurement and environmental concerns to records and clearance given to ineligible members, everything was found to be highly suspicious. This project violated the Indian environment ministry rules. The Comptroller and Audit General of India stated it was a classic example of the "fence eating the farm", or a case of the protector taking away what must be protected. This scam is a shameful case of how leading politicians, high-ranking military officials and influential bureaucrats colluded not for a common noble cause, but for selfish personal interests.
10. **IPL (Indian Premier League)** (2010) **Scam**—on the one hand, IPL has taken cricket to a new level altogether, and on the other hand, it has done more damage to

the image of cricket than one can imagine due to the heavy embezzlement involved in the bidding process of various franchisees. 2010 was definitely the year of shocking scams.

11. **Mining Scams**—Right from the illegal mining in Uttarakhand in the Ganga riverbed for stones and sand for construction work to the illegal iron ore mining and export scam in Karnataka, there was a series of mining scams that rocked the nation. These scams exemplify the strong nexus that exists between politicians, bureaucrats and mining barons. In places like Bellary, it is said that the entire government machinery is paid by the mining barons.
12. And the list goes on....

According to the Swiss Bank Report (2006), India topped the list of total amount held (deposits held by corrupt politicians, civil service officers and industrialists in the banks) and this amount was to the tune of 1,456 billion dollars, nations like Russia and UK followed in second place and third place respectively. The amount from India is about 13 times larger than the nation's foreign debt. And even today, India has more money in the Swiss tax haven than the rest of the world put together. It has been said that once this large loot of black money comes back to India, the entire foreign debt can be repaid in 24 hours.

Apart from the scandalously large share in Swiss Bank Accounts, the Indian tax evaders have deposited their black money in other tax havens like France, Dubai, USA, UK, etc.

Mossack Fonseca, a Panamanian law firm and corporate service provider, helped individuals worldwide to find ways to move their incomes into secret structures and jurisdictions to avoid payment of taxes. This law firm was at the centre of the Panama Papers Leak. Panama Papers investigation of 500 Indians (including actors, politicians, businessmen, etc.) as per new anti-black money law revealed the extent of violation, money laundering and tax evasion done in these cases.

> **Spotlight**
> The level of black money is a function of the integrity and honesty of both public officials/public organizations and private individuals/private organizations.

Table 9: Black Money Estimates in Developed and Developing Economies Period 1990-93

Economy	Parallel Economy (as % of GDP)
Developed Countries	
Germany, France, Great Britain, Sweden, Norway, Denmark, Ireland, and The Netherlands	13–23%
USA, Switzerland and Japan	8–10%
Spain, Portugal, Italy and Greece	24–30%
Developing Countries	
Brazil, Colombia, Venezuela and Chile	25–35%
Morocco and Tunisia	39–49%
Singapore and Honk Kong	13%

Source: http://www.crisil.com/youngthoughtleader/winners/topic4_Jyoti_Agarwal_Ilm_CAL.PDF

4.3 INDIAN BUSINESS AND BLACK MONEY

Many Indian businesses maintain benami firms or fake firms. Benami or fake firms are properties that are purchased in the names of others; the person who pays for the property does not buys it under her/his own name. The person on whose name the firm or property has been purchased is called 'benamdar' and the person who finances the deal is the real owner. For example, a typical black money operator sets up many firms to route money before it is invested. This is called 'layering' and this tactic helps in covering up the money trail. These firms are benami in nature and money is moved through jurisdiction areas where Indian laws are not recognized or accepted.

Crime syndicates are also into setting up businesses. They use such firms to convert their black money into white money. Offshore accounts also make it harder for authorities to nab these crime syndicates and wealthy individuals due to the lack of information and evidence. Moreover, these crime syndicates and wealthy individuals shelter their earnings in offshore accounts. Such unhealthy practices make it harder for honest people to rise up in life and moreover, these honest people have to pay higher taxes to make up for the tax revenue losses that are caused by these crime syndicates and wealthy individuals.

As discussed earlier, lobbying and political funding are one of the major sources of black money generated through the political-corporate nexus. According to statistics, of the 3452 candidates who contested more than one election from the period 2004 to 2013, 2967 candidates showed an increase in wealth and assets. Even business owners who want to contest elections offer exorbitant amounts to get tickets from political parties. These amounts are not reported in the financial statements of the political parties or the expenditure declarations of candidates.

Another tactic that the Indian businesses use is that of combining illicit money sources with legit ones, as this tactic makes it hard to detect their black money flows, especially if there is a large cash component involved in the legal business. Business owners also indulge in the practice of 'layering' which helps in covering the money transaction trail. In layering, the business owners open up many shell companies to route money before investing the same. A shell company is a non-trading firm set up with nominal paid-up capital and it is mainly used for financial frauds like tax evasion, loan diversion and black money generation. According to research statistics, Indian shell companies have laundered an amount worth 3,900 crore rupees in 2016. In the first half of 2017, the Enforcement Directorate (ED) conducted a massive raid operation against tax professionals, company secretaries and chartered accountants in an ongoing search operation under the Prevention of Money Laundering Act to seize black money channeled via such shell companies. There are approximately 40,000 unlisted companies in India alone, many of which often conceal their ownership and shareholding patterns through a network of related firms.

Spotlight

Another important factor that helps corporations to cover up the tracks of black money is a chain of various professionals based abroad, right from lawyers to chartered accountants. Indian businesses also siphon off money through many dummy firms and then channel it to trusts. Money and assets are seldom in the beneficiary's name and they are moved through jurisdictions where Indian regulations and laws are not recognized.

According to the Central Bureau of Investigation (CBI), in the past few years, 393 shell companies have diverted funds to the tune of 2,900 crore rupees and this money had been unearthed by the CBI during its probe into such cases over this time frame. These shell firms are spread across the nation and also across tax havens, which makes the investigation even more difficult. According to the CBI findings, these shell companies were being used for financial maneuverings in order to divert loan funds. These companies also used fake invoices and the practice of "round tripping" of funds to evade taxes, launder money and generate black money. Round tripping, also known as round trip transactions, is sending money abroad to tax havens in the guise of payments for fake imports through shell companies or hawala transactions, and then bringing back that money showing it as foreign investment, Global Depository Receipts (GDR), etc. *The Wall Street Journal* (WSJ is an American business-focused, English-language international daily newspaper) defines round tripping as "a form of barter that involves a company selling an unused asset to another company, while at the same time agreeing to buy back the same or similar assets at about the same price".

All theses black money practices by corporations clearly show low or no corporate governance levels.

4.4 MISUSE OF CORPORATE STRUCTURE AND ABUSE OF LAWS

The Vodafone tax case of 2012 is a glaring instance of the misuse of corporate structure for avoiding the payment of taxes. The Hutchison Group sold its entire business operation in India in 2007 to the Vodafone Group. The Hutchison Group had made investments in India during the period 1992-2006 via a number of subsidiaries each having separate corporate identity but in reality they were post box companies based in the British Virgin Islands, Cayman Islands and Mauritius. Such cases bring to light new methods of tax evasion. In this case, the trend called base erosion and profit shifting (BEPS) was brought to light. In BEPS, companies reduce the locally declared profits by shifting their profits to low or no tax locations and jurisdictions. After the 2012 Indian Supreme court ruling in favor of Vodafone, the Indian tax authority later on was arguing that Vodafone should have recovered the taxes from the Hutchison Group before sealing their deal. The tax authority further stated that though the deal was between two foreign corporations, yet the acquisitions of the underlying assets were in India. After the case, the Indian Government amended the tax laws with retrospective effect and again claimed taxes. In response to this, Vodafone filed a complaint with the international arbitration panel and the panel is yet to give its decision. Hence, the Indian Government has issued tax notice to the Hutchison Group. The Hutchison Group has expressed its objection by stating that it violates the principles of international law and moreover the Indian Supreme court has already ruled that the deal was not taxable in India. Such contradictory behaviors and actions by the Indian Government and tax authority send out mixed signals to the corporate world in particular and to the world in general. Although Vodafone won the Indian tax case of transfer pricing, the Indian Government and tax department need to ensure that everything is transparent or else even small players can be tempted to follow in the footsteps of their global counterparts. Also such global giants taking advantages of loopholes in legislations can affect the sincere domestic companies.

A Word of Caution

The corporate structure is also used to transfer illegal funds to foreign destinations. Corporations that misuse the corporate structure for generating black money are big crime syndicates in themselves.

We have already seen how shell companies (mis)use the corporate structure for money laundering. To keep a tab on shell companies, in 2017, a memorandum of understanding (MOU) for regular and automatic exchange of information was signed between the Ministry of Corporate Affairs and the Central Board of Direct Taxes. The provisions of this MOU facilitate the sharing of information related to audit reports of companies, PAN data, income tax returns, bank transactions, financial statements, etc., to carry out scrutiny, investigation and prosecution against such corporate criminals.

Companies also misuse corporate structure to establish public trusts and related trustee services for money laundering. They often donate money to trusts and NGOs for generating black money but often claim such donations as part of their tactic that the Indian businesses use (CSR) funds. Public trusts are the most preferred way to launder money as they are not sufficiently governed or monitored. Furthermore, in several places, there is no registration requirement, which makes trusts an ideal secrecy instrument for laundering money. Under the garb of CSR, corporations misuse corporate structure and norms to use charitable trusts, both internal and external, to falsify or fabricate their CSR spending. Moreover, CSR spending does not come under strict scrutiny or auditing; the laws in regards to CSR spending are not that strict in nature. For example, a rich businessman and his company under the CSR norms have to spend at least 20 crore rupees on CSR causes like education. The businessman would then issue a cheque (legal banking channel) in the name of a trust that works in the field of education. This trust after deducting its own commission and a cut for the middlemen would return the remaining sum in cash to its promoters (in this case the rich businessman). This process instantly converts the white money into black money. At the end of the year, the trust submits its report to the company that shares it under the CSR norms through the AOC-04 form containing the CSR spending details and the businessman and company get away with all the wrongdoings as the AOC-04 form is not scrutinized seriously or need not be examined by statutory auditors.

The Indian Government will have to come up with adequate provisions to ensure that CSR expenditure goes where it is officially meant to go, and strict implementation of the same is needed to eliminate the loose ends as far as CSR funds and CSR reporting are concerned. Moreover, whistle blowers that expose such misuse of corporate structure need to be protected. The real surgical strike will be when the nexus between politics and business is broken and also when all the related roadblocks are eliminated. Corporate structure and laws should be used for facilitating the growth of the company and the entire economy in a fair manner, but in today's times, it is seen misused more often than not.

4.5 MONEY LAUNDERING

Money laundering is the process used to disguise the source of money or assets derived from criminal activities like embezzlement, terrorist activity, illegal arms trafficking, insider trading, drug trafficking, etc. In other words, it refers to the conversion/movement/transfer of black money which has been illegally obtained in such a way that it appears to have originated from a legal source. This process helps the criminals and evaders to provide authenticate cover for their illegal source of income. Indians know this phenomenon as "hawala". Hawala predates the 'traditional' form of banking. Investopedia (Investopedia is the world's leading source of financial content on the web) defines money laundering as "The process of creating the appearance that large amounts of money obtained from serious crimes has originated from a legitimate source."

Money laundering or Hawala transactions severely affect the economic interests of the state. According to the Financial Action Task Force (FATF is an inter-governmental organization founded on the initiative of the G7 to develop policies to combat money laundering), money laundering is the processing of criminal proceeds to disguise their illegal origin. Laundering gives us a lopsided, misrepresented status of a nation, of an economy. Post-demonetization of November 2016, businesses and people with large hoards of high denomination turned to money laundering networks to convert their black money into white money; hence they were able to avoid apprehension by law or tax authorities successfully.

The word hawala comes from the Arabic root term 'hwl', which means to "transform" or "change". And in the case of black money, it means a parallel remittance system consisting of three main steps: placement, layering and integration. The first step of a hawala transaction is that the money launderer introduces the illegal income into the financial system, both formal and informal (placement). The second step is that of layering where the launderer does a series of conversions and transfers of the money through a series of transfers through various bank accounts, especially in tax havens like Switzerland and Dubai, purchase and sale of investment instruments like stocks and bonds, etc., to cover up the trail of its source (layering). The final step is that of returning the money into the legitimate economy through various ways like investing in luxury goods, real estate, etc., so that it can be extracted at a later date (integration). Hawala offers several ways of transforming money into various forms that make it appear legitimate, and this makes it a potential tool for both layering of money and also for integration of money. This entire process involves money transfer without any actual money movement.

Money laundering uses a network of hawala dealers or hawaladars. This money laundering system works through trusted connections and scrutiny-free remittance channels; hence though this system is risky, due to the trust factor it is efficient, effective and reliable. A hawala transaction takes place in one or two days; they are done in a short period of time as there is no delay caused due to weekends, holidays, etc. Hawala transactions are easy to carry out as there is no bureaucratic framework required, no identification required and moreover, the hawala transactions are cheaper (cost effective/low overheads) and there is either a confusing or no paper trail. The biggest motivating factor is that of tax evasion. Breaches of trust and honesty are rare. Sharing an example of money laundering through a hawala transaction: Firm 'A' on the outside appears to be a firm involved in the production of machinery, but on the inside, through a network of false corporate identities, this firm ships drugs concealed within the machinery to various foreign countries. Hawala is used to returns the proceeds of the drug sales back to the firm and its traffickers.

India plays a big (yet detrimental) role in Asia's illegal outflows—according to statistics, India contributes 10 percent of the billions illegally moved out of developing and emerging nations. 991.2 billion dollars were moved out of developing and emerging nations for crime, laundering, corruption and tax evasion. According to the International Monetary Fund (IMF), the turnover of this crime-based industry could be somewhere around 1.5 trillion dollars. Nearly 40 billion dollars of this is accounted for bribes paid to public officials in developing countries. According to the Transparency International reports of 2005 and 2008, about 62 percent and 40 percent respectively of Indians have paid bribes to get a job done in public offices. According to the Anti Money Laundering (AML) Basel Index 2013, Out of 140 countries, India has been ranked 93rd and 70th in 2012 and 2013 respectively with a score of 6.05 in 2012 and 5.95 in 2013. This score indicates that India is in the high-risk zone in the area of money laundering.

The dynamics of money laundering have become unpredictable and have evolved even more in the last few years due to advances in technology, more opportunities for international transactions and the expansion of international banks. Money laundering is not a new phenomenon for the Indian politicians and corporate world. It gained notoriety during the early 1990s when many of the Indian politicians were caught in its web.

A Word of Caution

The repercussion of money laundering is huge as it is not a crime that affects any particular person or group of persons, but it is a crime against nations and their economies, democratic institutions, financial markets, social and moral standards, and many other aspects.

4.6 TAX HAVENS

A tax haven, also called international financial centre or tax shelter, is a lucrative hub for the growing shadow or parallel economy. They have the following main characteristics that attract foreign investors: they have very low or no rates of taxation, they facilitate the setting up of trusts/foundations with ease, there is a lack of transparency in the operation of the tax system, they help their customers to get away from criminal liabilities, there are minimal or no disclosure requirements, and they help to easily launder illegal money.

Tax havens offer foreign individuals and corporations a cloak of concealment and confidentiality, minimal tax liability and large-scale profit shifting; a whole set of favorable financial advantages. These tax havens are the secret world of the global elite and high-net-worth individuals where large amounts of money are stashed away. Apart from the high and mighty, tax havens are used by multinational companies too. They help to move and reallocate taxable income from high-tax to low-tax jurisdiction offshore locations. A new study reveals Fortune 500 companies are holding nearly 2.5 trillion dollars in accumulated profits offshore to evade taxes.

The concept of parking illegal assets and money in tax havens started way back after the World War I. One of the most popular tax havens is Liechtenstein, initially called the island of penury, is a landlocked country between Switzerland and Austria. Although Liechtenstein is a tiny tax haven, yet it is very popular as it offers easy movement of illegal money and assets. Liechtenstein's tagline is "invest like a prince" and it set the trend of tax havens. While small in size, Liechtenstein is considered a giant as far as tax havens are concerned and it is closely linked with the parallel international business economy. Thereafter several safe territories like Monaco, the Virgin Islands, etc., also began to offer safe vaults/safe parking places for black money.

Globalization has led to the erosion of business boundaries but when it comes to tax laws they are still being implemented locally. This aspect is taken (dis)advantage of by individuals and corporations, who use the wings of globalization to fly off their black money into offshore tax havens. The lack of high quality governance and oversight institutions is yet another factor that allows such affluent tax havens to operate in an unhindered fashion. Tax evading companies through options like royalty payments, intra-firm trade, etc., can set up units in tax havens and use them to avoid their home country taxes.

The Organization for Economic Cooperation and Development (OECD is an intergovernmental economic organization with an aim to promote policies that will improve the social and economic well-being of people around the world) lists four key factors in considering whether a nation/jurisdiction is a tax haven or not. These four key factors include nominal or no tax, lack of transparency, lack of administrative laws, and absence of a requirement that the activity be substantial.

> **Spotlight**
>
> Tax havens are locations where the regulatory environment is liberal and individuals and corporations can set up proxy business units or conduit companies which can appear as authentic business units without really doing any real commercial activity, and this is possible in such tax havens as there are very few registration and judicial barriers.

Tax havens also usually offer strong secrecy regarding income, wealth and accounts, and this makes them very attractive locations for safe keeping of unaccounted wealth and assets. Some of the tax havens popular among Indians are Switzerland, Dubai, Monaco, Liechtenstein, etc. Dubai provides its customers with discreet services, secrecy, security and privacy. In today's world of globalization, several big corporations maintain billions of dollars in offshore accounts in such tax havens to minimize corporate taxes. In the year 2009, when global recession was at its peak, the US had suffered a major loss in terms of billions of dollars to these tax havens. According to a 2016 report by Citizens for Tax Justice, 367 companies in the Fortune 500 operate subsidiaries in tax-haven nations around the globe. The most popular tax haven among the Fortune 500 companies is the Netherlands. Other tax havens include the Channel Islands, Singapore, Mauritius, the Bahamas and Bermuda.

Panama is yet another popular tax haven—there are firms in Panama that can help set up a company within 48 hours and provide nominee directors and shareholders in a short time period. It was recently all over the news for the massive data leak of more than 11.5 million financial and legal documents from Mossack Fonseca, a Panamanian law firm. They were initially obtained by a German newspaper *Süddeutsche Zeitung* and subsequently became the subject of a year-long investigation by the International Consortium of Investigative Journalists (ICIJ is a Washington-based international network that performs cross-border watchdog journalism). Many of the involved entities were reportedly found to be shell companies in order to cover up their business dealings worth billions of dollars. Such shell companies provided layers of proxies that help in money laundering and tax rationalization. Several operators were involved that controlled hundreds of companies and firms.

The Panama Papers is the biggest data leak in the world history; an unprecedented leak of 11.5 million files containing information dating back several decades from the world's fourth biggest offshore law firm, Mossack Fonseca. It outnumbers the combined total of Swiss leaks, Luxembourg tax files, Wikileaks and Offshore leaks, and gives a never-before-seen view inside the offshore world. These files and documents were leaked to the German daily, *Süddeutsche Zeitung*, which then shared them with the Washington-based International Consortium of Investigative Journalists, the British Broadcasting Corporation and other media organizations. This massive leak exposed to the world how law firms, banks, politicians, drug traffickers, celebrities and billionaires worked in unison to build an intricate system through black money, criminal activities, money laundering and offshore firms. The files and documents list approximately 15,600 paper companies that banks created for people who wanted to keep their incomes concealed, including thousands set up by global banking giants like HSBC and UBS. One out of every two companies appearing in the leaked Mossack Fonseca documents was incorporated in the British

Virgin Islands. This is followed by Panama in the second spot and the Bahamas in the third sport, according to the findings based on the Panama Papers; shared in the following table.

Table 10: The 10 Most Popular Tax Havens in the Panama Papers

Rank	Tax Haven
1	British Virgin Islands
2	Panama
3	The Bahamas
4	Seychelles
5	Niue
6	Samoa
7	British Anguilla
8	Nevada
9	Hong Kong
10	The United Kingdom

Source: panamapapers.icij.org

Studies have shown that about one-third of the global wealth is beyond authoritative purview and outside the reach of tax laws and regulations. Currently, there are numerous tax havens across the globe and their number has reached more than 90.

4.7 CHAPTER RECAP

1. The magnitude and evilness of black money in India can be measured through its effects. The ever-expanding magnitude of black money still continues to haunt the Indian landscape.

2. A variety of methods are used for deriving the magnitude, estimates and statistics of black money, both in India and on a global level, but each source results in the generation of divergent estimates and statistics. There are several methods like circulation velocity method, input-output ratio method, and sampling method to arrive at black money estimates.

3. According to the Government of India (2012), the extent of black money is somewhere between $500 billion and $1400 billion. Other estimates include an average of ₹ 1,36,466 crore or $27.3 billion stashed annually during 2002 to 2006; which means about ₹ 6,92,328 crore or $136.5 billion hoarded in the five-year period (Global Financial Integrity Report, 2006), ₹ 9,295 crore stashed in Swiss banks by Indians (White Paper, Government of India), a World Bank report puts India's shadow economy at close to one-fifth of economic output, and many more such shocking statistics are shared in various national and international reports, books, surveys and findings.

4. Tax havens play a crucial role in the generation of illicit financial flows. As tax havens provide opportunities to wealthy individuals and corporations to evade taxes, escape tax scrutiny, secrecy and anonymity provisions, and have very low tax rates, makes them profitable locations for illicit financial flows.

5. According to the Interpol estimates, the size of hawala done by Indian operators is pegged at possibly 40 percent of the nation's Gross Domestic Product.

6. In the last 40+ years, India has lost at least 17 trillion rupees to tax havens. India has exported goods and services worth at least 17 trillion rupees over the past four decades but did not remit an equivalent amount in foreign exchange.

7. Apart from the scandalously large share in Swiss Bank Accounts, the Indian tax evaders have deposited their black money in other tax havens like France, Dubai, USA, UK, etc.

8. Many Indian businesses maintain benami firms or fake firms. Benami or fake firms are properties that are purchased in the names of others; the person who pays for the property does not buys it under her/his own name. The person on whose name the firm or property has been purchased is called 'benamdar' and person who finances the deal is the real owner.

9. Another tactic that the Indian businesses use is that of combining illicit money sources with legit ones, as this tactic makes it hard to detect their black money flows, especially if there is a large cash component involved in the legal business.

10. Business owners also indulge in the practice of 'layering' which helps in covering the money transaction trail. In layering, the business owners open up many shell companies to route money before investing the same. A shell company is a non-trading firm set up with nominal paid-up capital and it is mainly used for financial frauds like tax evasion, loan diversion and black money generation.

11. According to the Central Bureau of Investigation (CBI), in the past few years, 393 shell companies have diverted funds to the tune of 2,900 crore rupees and this money had been unearthed by the CBI during its probe into such cases over this time frame.

12. Corporations that misuse the corporate structure for generating black money are big crime syndicates in themselves. Corporate structure and laws should be used for facilitating the growth of the company and the economy in a fair manner, but in today's time, it is seen misused more often than not.

13. Money laundering is the process used to disguise the source of money or assets derived from criminal activities like embezzlement, terrorist activity, illegal arms trafficking, insider trading, drug trafficking, etc. In other words, it refers to the conversion/movement/transfer of black money which has been illegally obtained in such a way that it appears to have originated from a legal source.

14. The word hawala comes from the Arabic root term 'hwl', which means to "transform" or "change". And in the case of black money, it means a parallel remittance system consisting of three main steps: placement, layering and integration.

15. India plays a big (yet detrimental) role in Asia's illegal outflows—according to statistics, India contributes 10 percent of the billions illegally moved out of developing and emerging nations.

16. A tax haven, also called international financial centre or tax shelter, is a lucrative hub for the growing shadow or parallel economy. Tax havens offer foreign individuals and corporations a cloak of concealment and confidentiality, minimal tax liability and large-scale profit shifting; a whole set of favorable financial advantages.

17. The concept of parking illegal assets and money in tax havens started way back after the World War I. One of the most popular tax havens is Liechtenstein, initially called the island of penury, is a landlocked country between Switzerland and Austria.

18. Panama is yet another popular tax haven—there are firms in Panama that can help set up a company within 48 hours and provide nominee directors and shareholders in a short time period. It was recently all over the news for the massive data leak of more than 11.5 million financial and legal documents from Mossack Fonseca, a Panamanian law firm.

19. Studies have shown that about one-third of the global wealth is beyond authoritative purview and outside the reach of tax laws and regulations. Currently, there are numerous tax havens across the globe and their number has reached more than 90.

4.8 QUESTIONS FOR REFLECTION

1. What roles do the tax havens play in the generation of black money?
2. What happens when black money comes back to India?
3. How much of Indian black money is floating around?
4. What are the three main processes involved in money laundering?
5. What is the impact of black money on the Indian economy?
6. What is the role of Financial Action Task Force?
7. How big is the Panama Papers leak?

PART 3

Measures for Curbing Black Money in India

Chapter 5

Black Money Across the Globe

Black money is prevalent in both developed and developing nations. Dealing with the issue of black money and illegal assets held by Indians in foreign banks and tax havens is more complex, as it involves international laws and also it depends on the response in terms of cooperation or non-cooperation from the foreign nations. Largest companies on the global map have huge sums parked in tax havens. These companies manufacture, market and sell the most, but at the same time, they pay the least in terms of their tax dues. There has never been as much money held offshore as there is today. In the past 5+ years, the amount of money in tax havens has increased over 25 percent.

The issue of black money has been a matter of serious political debate not just in India, but in the world too. According to the International Monetary Fund study, "Countries with relatively low tax rates, fewer laws and regulations, and a well-established rule of law tend to have smaller shadow economies." All the estimates from the various sources and studies shared in here may vary from one another, but each of these estimates is a large number, and this is what is alarming.

5.1 GLOBAL BLACK MONEY STATISTICS

There are 90+ tax havens in the world with Switzerland being one of the main players. According to 2015 statistics, foreign wealth held in Switzerland reached 2.3 trillion dollars. Before the Panama Papers leak occurred, according to Indian government's statistics, one trillion dollars of Indian black money was believed to be stashed away in offshore locations. Setting up business in the Cayman Islands and Singapore is quite easy, which makes them perfect places for corporations to conceal or evade a major portion of their money through shell companies and subsidiaries. The British Virgin Islands have a relaxed tax regime with virtually no taxes and this makes it a lucrative tax haven. From 2012 through 2014, overseas investment by Indians grew by an astounding 700 percent in the British Virgin Islands. All the tax havens function in unison as one large network of illegal/evaded money and assets management. The outflow of black money from Mexico between 2004 and 2013 stood at 528.4 billion dollars, which is just a little more than that from India. According to the latest estimates shared by the Bank of Italy, between six and seven trillion dollars worth of black money is sheltered in tax havens across the globe.

Table 11: Financial Secrecy Index, 2015

Rank	Jurisdiction	FSI Value	Secrecy Score	Global Scale Weight
1	Switzerland	1,466.1	73	5.625
2	Hong Kong	1,259.4	72	3.842
3	United States	1,254.8	60	19.603
4	Singapore	1,147.1	69	4.280
5	Cayman Islands	1,013.2	65	4.857
6	Luxembourg	817.0	55	11.630
7	Lebanon	760.2	79	0.377
8	Germany	701.9	56	6.026
9	Bahrain	471.4	74	0.164
10	UAE	440.8	77	0.085

Source: Tax Justice Network

According to the 2015 Financial Secrecy Index released by the Tax Justice Network, a comprehensive survey on global financial secrecy, Switzerland is on the number one position, followed by Hong Kong and the United States. This survey included more than 90 jurisdictions. The survey findings go to show that secrecy is valued over everything else; these jurisdictions under their secrecy provisions help people to escape rules and laws. There is a clear unwillingness in the global community to engage in effective information exchange.

Immigrants without legal status often find themselves employed in the parallel or underground economy. They do not report their incomes for fear of being deported by authorities due to their illegal status. Another aspect for many people joining the underground economy is due to the lack of full-time jobs. Rules and regulations that make it mandatory for employers to pay social welfare and health benefits to their employees may make the employers to keep a certain quota of employees unreported/off the records. Such scenarios are found on all points of the world compass.

According to findings by Edgar Feige, an emeritus professor of economics at the University of Wisconsin-Madison, underground economic activity in the United States totaled two trillion dollars in 2012, approximately 12 percent of the GDP. In 2011, the United States lost approximately 39.8 billion dollars in tax revenues due to corporations and individuals who hid their money in tax havens. According to the Internal Revenue Service (IRS is the revenue service of the United States Federal Government) estimates, nearly 500 billion dollars in taxes were lost in 2012 due to unreported wages.

As per the 2012 estimates by the Global Financial Integrity (GFI), Russia was on the top of the list with 122.86 billion dollars, followed by China, in terms of the quantum of black money moving out of a nation. As per the 2014 estimates revealed in the Annual Global Update on Illicit Financial Flows report on cumulative illicit outflows from developing economies for ten years between 2003 and 2012 by GFI, China topped the list with 1.25 trillion dollars, followed by Russia with 973.86 billion dollars and Mexico with 514.26 billion dollars. In this same list, India appeared on the fourth position with 439.59 billion dollars worth illicit money that has moved out of India in this ten-year period.

According to a report by the Bank of England, no more than half of the banknotes in circulation are being used for legitimate purposes and the remaining half of the banknotes are used to fund the black economy or stashed away abroad. Another statistic stated by the Bank of England is that now there is an equivalent of around £1,000 banknotes in circulation for each person in the United Kingdom. The equivalent figures for Australia (£1,220) and the United States (£2,500) are higher. According to the bank as much a £3 billion could be hidden indoors with an average of £345 per hoarder; this is why the demand for banknotes is becoming higher and higher. According to the latest figures, the United Kingdom accounted for the largest share of approximately 359 Swiss Francs (over 25 percent) of the total foreign money with Swiss banks. According to the findings of the Institute of Economic Affairs (IEA is a think tank that promotes free market economics), Britain's black market accounts for about 10 percent of the economy or more than £150 billion a year, and about 30 million people are employed in the shadow economy across the European Union. In 2007, the black market stood at 12.2 percent of the British economy and shrank to 10.9 percent in 2008. However, in 2011 it grew slightly to 11 percent before falling again to 10.3 percent. The shadow economy in Britain is relatively small as compared to many other European nations.

According to the Australian Bureau of Statistics (ABS is an independent statistical agency of the Government of Australia), in 2013, black money which included proceeds from illegal activities as well as other areas is estimated to be at 2.1 percent of GDP. This report also stated that black money is typically concentrated in industries such as "construction, accommodation, cafes and restaurants, personal and other services, and retail trade".

> **A Word of Caution**
>
> All these estimates reveal one glaring fact—they all show just how unequal the world is!

5.1.1 More Global Statistics

Holding a foreign bank account is not illegal in France, but failing to disclose the fact is. In 2008, the French Government received a list of 1,27,000 names of French account holders with HSBC. Later on, it was found that the original list had been tampered with and several names had gone missing from it. Apparently, this political censorship was done by the French authorities in order to avoid public revelation of certain names (who could be potential tax evaders and fraudsters) as this would adversely affect the public image of the political class. In 2016, France received a list with 3,80,000 accounts and 12 billion worth of black money stashed away by wealthy clients in the UBS Bank in Switzerland.

Small players are also playing this big game. Citing a few examples of how small countries get dragged into this wicked web. The Organized Crime and Corruption Reporting Project (OCCRP) exposed an immense financial fraud scheme that enabled vast sums to be pumped out of Russia; this scam is called the Russian Laundromat. Large amounts of black money were moved out of Russia through money laundering, bribery, banks and exploitation of loose ends in the Moldovian laws. Recently, OCCRP obtained details of more than 120 bank accounts connected to this scam. Authorities in Moldova, the United Kingdom, Latvia and Russia continue to investigate the Laundromat, but attempts to bring culprits to justice are thwarted due to lack of cooperation from Russian officials. This scam involves fake companies and most of them were registered in London at Companies House. Typically, company A loaned a large sum of money to company B, and other companies in Russia, fronted by Moldovians would guarantee these loans. Thereafter, company B would fail to return the money and Moldovian judges would authentic such debt. This would allow Russian companies to transfer the real money to banks in Moldova and Latvia. The money generated through this scam went everywhere; it involved 96 countries, both small and big, through a network of hidden offshore administrations and the global shadow financial system.

Recent statistics by the International Consortium of Investigative Journalists (ICIJ) shows that 5.38 billion rupees was deposited in the HSBC Bank in Switzerland. According to the ICIJ report titled: “The Swiss Leaks”, Nepali nationals had used 36 bank accounts to deposit the black money. After India,

Pakistan and Sri Lanka, Nepal ranks fourth in South Asia in terms of deposit volume.

According to the World Bank data, the total bribes paid each year equals to about 1,000 billion dollars, representing 9% of the global trade. Statistics also reveal that on a global scale, 8 percent of the financial wealth of households is held in tax havens.

5.2 FOREIGN COUNTERMEASURES

There are ongoing discussions, dialogs and diplomatic endeavors among the nations in the international taxation sphere in regards to how to implement robust tax policy and administration, and how to deal with the black money flows and the growing number of tax havens and their impact on the taxation structure. Details about these global countermeasures that India and other nations are an integral part of and through which all these nations are trying to curb this cancer are shared in the following paragraphs.

The Tax Information Exchange Agreements (TIEAs) facilitate the exchange of information relating to a particular criminal or civil tax investigation. TIEAs are by request only; information will only be provided and exchanged between the signatories only if a proper request is made based on the agreement provisions. TIEAs are broadly based on the Organization for Economic Cooperation and Development Model Agreement on Exchange of Information on tax matters. With rising cross-border capital flows, the exchange of information between nations is gaining importance in the international agenda. TIEAs also support the aims of the OECD's Harmful Tax Practices Initiative. Double Tax Avoidance Agreement (DTAAs) deals with the aspect of double taxation in order to encourage cross-national economic activities and foreign investment. Their main purpose is to eliminate or avoid double taxation of the income earned from the source country as well as the residence country. Double taxation is the levying of tax by two or more jurisdictions on the same declared income. The chaos caused by conflicting country specific tax rules is taken care of by DTAAs and their provisions for handling taxation of international incomes. DTAAs provide specific guidelines on how the income is to be taxed by the source and resident countries. Any jurisdiction with 12 or more such agreements is considered as cooperative and accordingly it is taken off from the OECD list of non-committing countries.

The United States of America has an extensive computerized system for tax tracking in place. The US also has a scheme of national identity involving the assignment of an account number to every taxpayer and this account number is called the Social Security Number. This computerized system includes a national computer center with regional computer centers to collect and collate data related to corporate shareholdings from all corporates, financial bonds, bank accounts, etc., and then this data is used to compare with the amounts shared by taxpayers in their return forms. Taxpayers are bound to feel vulnerable as they all have to declare all their financial data and incomes from various sources, or else they could be exposed by the process of comparisons made by the computer system. Similar such computerized systems are set up in other nations like Australia, the United Kingdom, etc.

The United States federal legislation, the Foreign Account Tax Compliance Act (FATCA), is meant to reduce tax evasion by the nation's citizens, tax residents and entities. All of them are required to report their worldwide income to the Internal Revenue Service (IRS) whether they live in the States or not. The main purpose of FATCA is to detect and deter the evasion of national taxes by US persons who hide money outside the country, and to promote cross-border tax compliance. The FATCA is a part of the unrelated jobs legislation known as the HIRE law. Under the India-US agreement that came into force in 2015, India can give information to the US on 'high value accounts' of US residents in India that have a balance of more than one million dollars.

Harmful Tax Competition Initiative was introduced by the Organization for Economic Cooperation and Development (OECD) in 1998. Now it is called the Harmful Tax Practices Initiative and it is part of a wider initiative of the member countries to promote good governance in a global economy.

Its main aim is to promote an environment in which a fair and transparent tax competition is possible.

Another important measure is the draft Anti-money Laundering rules approved by the European Parliament, which stipulated that the ultimate owners of trusts and companies would have to be listed in public registers in the European Union. Adequate, accurate and up-to-date information relating to the beneficial owners has to be maintained by the member states. The Fourth Anti-Money Laundering Directive (AML), 2015, takes into account the new recommendations adopted by the Financial Action Task Force (FATF) in 2012, which the European Union member states have committed to follow. FATF is a coordinated international response and effort against the rising menace of money laundering. AML aims to safeguard the interests of financial and credit institutions against risks like terrorism financing and money laundering. It aims to protect the interests of the society, to strengthen the internal market, and to safeguard the economic and financial stability of the European Union. The proposed Fifth Anti-Money Laundering Directive amends the fourth one to include more provisions and norms to increase transparency related to beneficial ownership and to control terrorism financing. India too is a member of FATF and other anti-money laundering bodies like the Eurasian Group on Combating Money Laundering and Financing of Terrorism, the Asia/Pacific Group on Money Laundering, the Egmont Group, etc.

The foreign countermeasures toolbox includes the United Nation Convention on Forbidding Drug trafficking. China has always given great importance to fighting against black money and preventing money laundering. China acceded to the United Nation Convention on Forbidding Drug trafficking and has taken the obligation of prescribing money laundering as a crime subjected to severe punishment and penalties in its substantial laws and regulations.

Canada's Anti-Tax Haven Initiative, 2007, aims to improve tax fairness and to curb the extent to which tax avoidance structures are used to avoid domestic taxes. It aims to do this by implementing various measures to prevent multinational corporations from using tax havens and other tax avoidance techniques like tower structure and double dipping. In the double dipping technique, corporations create double deduction/double benefits for a single foreign investment (same source).

The Global Forum on Transparency and Exchange of Information for Tax Purposes is a multilateral framework that works under the sponsorship and support of the OECD and the G20. Its main aim is to ensure a rapid and effective implementation of the standards on transparency and exchange of information for tax purposes. It deals with areas of tax havens, tax evasion, double taxation, money laundering and tax information exchange agreements. This forum was restructured in 2009 in response to the G20 call to strengthen implementation of these standards. Through in-depth peer reviews, this forum ensures that its members fully implement the standards and norms of transparency and exchange of information.

In 2003, the first legally binding international anti-corruption instrument came into being—the United Nations Convention Against Corruption (UNCAC). UNCAC is a major step in promoting international cooperation against corruption including crimes related to black money. The member-countries are bound to provide mutual legal assistance in the prosecution of offenders as well as in tracing, freezing and confiscating the proceeds of corruption. India ratified the UNCAC in 2011. India also ratified yet another UN Convention in 2011, the United Nations Convention Against Transnational Organized Crime (UNTOC). UNTOC is the first comprehensive and global legally binding instrument to fight transnational organized crimes of money laundering, arms trafficking, etc. The United Nations Convention Against Transnational Organized Crime (UNTOC) was adopted in 2000 and it is the key international instrument in the fight against transnational organized crime. If corruption and crime go international, so must legislation and enforcement. UNTOC requires state parties to incorporate the offence of money laundering into their national criminal law.

There are several other legal frameworks like the Inter-American Convention Against Corruption, OECD Convention on Combating Bribery of Foreign Public Officials in International Business Transactions, etc., which are striving hard to establish robust anti-corruption standards on a global level.

> **A Word of Caution**
>
> All these international measures are needed to be implemented in spirit. One of the main downsides of these international tax treaties and agreements involving more than two nations is that they normally face a lot of problems and differences of interests; hence at times it becomes difficult to implement and follow-up certain provisions.

5.2.1 More Global Measures

Besides international tax treaties like Tax Information Exchange Agreements, Double Taxation Avoidance Agreements and Multilateral Convention on Mutual Administrative Assistance in Tax Matters, the Common Reporting Standards (CRS) also plays an important role in the automatic exchange of tax and financial information on a global level in order to fight tax evasion and improve tax compliance. CRS is the agreed global standard for automatic exchange of information and it is approved by the Organization for Economic Cooperation and Development. CRS is applicable to all types of financial accounts like business accounts, investments, etc. According to the CRS guidelines, reporting financial institutions (RFIs) will comply with local legislation to identify and report information on reportable accounts to their local tax authorities on a yearly basis. In turn, the local tax authorities will exchange information with other reportable jurisdictions with whom they have entered into automatic exchange of information agreements.

India signed an agreement with the US to improve global tax compliance, promote transparency between the two countries on tax matters, and to implement the US Foreign Account Tax Compliance Act (FATCA) in 2015. Further to this agreement, both the countries signed the Competent Authority Agreement and Notification (CAA) to initiate the automatic exchange of information related to tax matters.

The OECD Base Erosion and Profit Shifting (BEPS) initiative is an inclusive framework with over 100 nations and jurisdictions that are collaborating to implement a worldwide framework of BEPS measures in order to tackle BEPS. In the year 2013, OECD and G20 nations, adopted a 15-point Action Plan to deal with BEPS. BEPS refers to tax planning and avoidance techniques and strategies used by multinational companies in order to evade taxes or reduce tax burden in their own country by exploiting gaps in tax laws to artificially shift profits to low or no-tax locations. Such multinational companies can gain competitive advantages over companies that operate only at the domestic level.

The financial intelligence unit, TRACFIN, is the French anti-money laundering unit associated with the Ministry of Finances. It conducts a money laundering, illicit financial circuits and terrorist financing risk assessment every year. These assessments are based on the money laundering and terrorist financing risk assessment method set out by the Financial Action Task Force. Through such assessments, TRACFIN is able to unearth information and facts that assist in identifying suspicious cases related to money laundering, organized crime, terrorism funding, etc. TRACFIN also conducts awareness-raising initiatives and publishes case studies on its online portal to educate people. This unit also represents France in bilateral agreements and international organizations that are engaged in the fight against money laundering and terrorist funding. In its 2016 activity report, TRACFIN claimed to have processed 64,815 reported information in the form of suspicious transaction reports; TRACFIN had never seen such a rise since its inception. It is associated with groups and networks like the Egmont Group of Financial Intelligence Units and the Camden Assets Recovery Inter-Agency Network (CARIN) for the fight against money laundering. The Egmont Group is a united group of several Financial Intelligence Units that provides a trusted platform for exchange of financial intelligence, expertise and information in order to curb money laundering and terrorist financing. CARIN is an informal network of practitioners and experts in all aspects related to asset tracing, freezing, seizure and confiscation of the proceeds of crime. CARIN acts as an advisory group to similar networks and it promotes the exchange of good practices and exchange of information. All these groups, networks and frameworks have one major goal of improving cross-border cooperation in order to deprive criminal elements from enjoying their illicit incomes and illicit profits.

> **Spotlight**
>
> Flushing out black money and its perpetrators is a long haul. Most of these global measures have everything in place, right from integration of information through information technology to capacity building. What is needed to bring all these aspects into action is constant cooperation among all these groups, networks and frameworks. They need to facilitate and expand the exchange of timely information in order to clamp down on black money.

5.3 CHAPTER RECAP

1. The issue of black money has been a matter of serious political debate not just in India, but in the world too.

2. There are 90+ tax havens in the world with Switzerland being one of the main players. According to 2015 statistics, foreign wealth held in Switzerland reached 2.3 trillion dollars.

3. All the tax havens function in unison as one large network of illegal/evaded money and assets management.

4. According to the latest estimates shared by the Bank of Italy, between six and seven trillion dollars worth of black money is sheltered in tax havens across the globe.

5. According to the 2015 Financial Secrecy Index released by the Tax Justice Network, a comprehensive survey on global financial secrecy, Switzerland is on the number one position, followed by Hong Kong and the United States. This survey included more than 90 jurisdictions. The survey findings go to show that secrecy is valued over everything else; these jurisdictions under their secrecy provisions help people to escape rules and laws. There is a clear unwillingness in the global community to engage in effective information exchange.

6. According to findings by Edgar Feige, an emeritus professor of economics at the University of Wisconsin—Madison, underground economic activity in the United States totaled two trillion dollars in 2012, approximately 12 percent of the GDP.

7. As per the 2012 estimates by the Global Financial Integrity (GFI), Russia was on the top of the list with 122.86 billion dollars, followed by China, in terms of the quantum of black money moving out of a nation.

8. According to a report by the Bank of England, no more than half of the banknotes in circulation are being used for legitimate purposes and the remaining half of the banknotes are used to fund the black economy or stashed away abroad.

9. According to the Australian Bureau of Statistics (ABS is an independent statistical agency of the Government of Australia), in 2013, black money which included proceeds from illegal activities as well as other areas is estimated to be at 2.1 percent of GDP.

10. According to the World Bank data, the total bribes paid each year equals to about 1,000 billion dollars, representing 9% of the global trade.

11. The Tax Information Exchange Agreements (TIEAs) facilitate the exchange of information relating to a particular criminal or civil tax investigation. TIEAs are by request only; information will only be provided and exchanged between the signatories only if a proper request is made based on the agreement provisions. Double Tax Avoidance Agreement (DTAA) deals with the aspect of double taxation in order to encourage cross-national economic activities and foreign investment. Their main purpose is to eliminate or avoid double taxation of the income earned from the source country as well as the residence country.

12. The United States of America has an extensive computerized system for tax tracking in place. The US also has a scheme of national identity involving the assignment of an account number to every taxpayer and this account number is called the Social Security Number. This computerized system includes a national computer center with regional computer centers to collect and collate data related to corporate shareholdings from all corporates, financial bonds, bank accounts, etc., and then this data is used to compare with the amounts shared by taxpayers in their return forms.

13. The United States federal legislation, the Foreign Account Tax Compliance Act (FATCA), is meant to reduce tax evasion by the nation's citizens, tax residents and entities.

14. Harmful Tax Competition Initiative was introduced by the Organization for Economic Cooperation and Development (OECD) in 1998. Now it is called the Harmful Tax Practices Initiative and it is part of a wider initiative of the member countries to promote good governance in a global economy. Its main aim is to promote an environment in which a fair and transparent tax competition is possible.

15. Another important measure is the draft Anti-money Laundering rules approved by the European Parliament, which stipulated that the ultimate owners of trusts and companies would have to be listed in public registers in the European Union. Adequate, accurate and up-to-date information relating to the beneficial owners has to be maintained by the member states.

16. Canada's Anti-Tax Haven Initiative, 2007, aims to improve tax fairness and to curb the extent to which tax avoidance structures are used to avoid domestic taxes.

17. The Global Forum on Transparency and Exchange of Information for Tax Purposes is a multilateral framework that works under the sponsorship and support of the OECD and the G20. Its main aim is to ensure a rapid and effective implementation of the standards on transparency and exchange of information for tax purposes.

18. In 2003, the first legally binding international anti-corruption instrument came into being—the United Nations Convention Against Corruption (UNCAC). UNCAC is a major step in promoting international cooperation against corruption including crimes related to black money.

19. Besides international tax treaties like Tax Information Exchange Agreements, Double Taxation Avoidance Agreements and Multilateral Convention on Mutual Administrative Assistance in Tax Matters, the Common Reporting Standards (CRS) also plays an important role in the automatic exchange of tax and financial information on a global level in order to fight tax evasion and improve tax compliance.

20. The OECD Base Erosion and Profit Shifting (BEPS) initiative is an inclusive framework with over 100 nations and jurisdictions that are collaborating to implement a worldwide framework of BEPS measures in order to tackle BEPS.

21. The financial intelligence unit, TRACFIN, is the French anti-money laundering unit associated with the Ministry of Finances. It conducts a money laundering, illicit financial circuits and terrorist financing risk assessment every year.

22. All these groups, networks and frameworks have one major goal of improving cross-border cooperation in order to deprive criminal elements from enjoying their illicit incomes and illicit profits.

5.4 QUESTIONS FOR REFLECTION

1. How have the various global measures affected the levels of corruption and black money?
2. What is the main role of TRACFIN?
3. How do the OECD and the G20 contribute in the global fight against black money?
4. What implications do the global black money statistics have?
5. What is the role of the Common Reporting Standards?
6. List at least three international instruments against black money along with their advantages?

Chapter 6

The Way Forward

The earlier chapters have made it clear that the menace of black money is deep and complex and there is no single panacea that can rid society of this menace. India and all its stakeholders need to adopt a multi-pronged, well-coordinated approach. Apart from rationalization of tax rates, what is also needed to make this approach more effective is effective implementation of tax laws and necessary changes in public perception about tax evasion and black money.

The main weakness of all anti-black money programs and methods is that they touch the problem of black money already created but they do not go into the root cause of the generation of black money. The key element of tackling this huge problem of black money includes prevention of generation of black money, effective detection of black money, foolproof investigation and immediate justice.

One of the most important ways of curbing black money is through setting up of robust information exchange systems. This aspect is not that prevalent in the various departments of the Indian Government. This lacuna leads to loopholes that facilitate black money hoarders and tax evaders to carry on with their spurious activities in a bold and unchecked manner. Their black money leads to investment in unproductive assets like luxurious houses, precious jewelry, lavish parties, expensive yachts, etc.

The Finance Bill's amendments in 2017 to the Income Tax Act come with a lot of controversial changes, especially in regards to political funding. According to the new provisions of this bill, people can make use of the "electoral bonds" to donate to political parties anonymously, and the cap of how much an individual or a company can donate to political parties has been removed. Such amendments defeat the very purpose and effectiveness of any fight launched against black money.

Several measures have been suggested over the years by various commission and committees. The Wanchoo Committee also known as the Direct Taxes Enquiry Committee—report on tax evasion and black money (1971), National Institute of Public Finance and Policy report (Aspects of the Black Economy in India, 1985), Indirect Taxation Enquiry Committee (1978), Tax Reforms Committee (1992), White Paper on Black Money (2012) and many more have suggested measures, but these measures were either not implemented or were implemented merely on paper.

6.1 PAST AND RECENT MEASURES TO KEEP BLACK MONEY IN CHECK

A number of Voluntary Disclosure Schemes have been announced from time to time since 1951. In the 1951 scheme, tax laws were relaxed in an attempt to persuade tax evaders to come forward with the unaccounted income. Thereafter, two schemes were announced: the first scheme was called "60-40" wherein any tax evader who disclosed her/his unaccounted income paid 60 percent of the disclosed income and 40 percent was accounted into the books; the second scheme was called "block scheme" wherein instead of a flat rate of 60 percent, different tax rates were applied based on the blocks of undisclosed income. These schemes were criticized as critics and experts thought these schemes favored the fraudulent persons at the cost of honest taxpayers. Despite this criticism, yet another scheme was declared in 1975 which targeted unaccounted income, concealed wealth and undervalued assets. The 1975 scheme was quite successful in comparison to the earlier schemes mainly due to the factor of fear psychology that was caused by the emergency in the same year. The findings that came to light during schemes showed that a considerable percentage of income disclosed were kept as holdings in bank accounts within the country.

Demonetization has been done in the past too to curb the menace of black money. In 1946, the then Indian Government had demonetized hundred rupee notes. The people were given a time limit to exchange the demonetized notes at the Reserve Bank of India or its authorized agencies. Rigorous investigation was carried out on the declarations regarding the sources of income and the exchange was not allowed if the people failed to provide valid reasons for their incomes. This caused a lot of inconvenience to the people and moreover, this measure was not that successful. Again in 1978, the then Indian Government announced demonetization of 1,000, 5,000 and 10,000 denomination currency notes. Again people were given a time limit to exchange their notes at the Reserve Bank of India and its branches, and this exchange was allowed when they were able to give clear explanation for the source of these notes along with the time and manner of acquisition and also valid attestation of identity. This demonetization drive gave better results than the previous one of 1946. Such frequent drives have a limited impact as the black money players have the means and network to convert their high denomination notes into lower denomination notes. Thereafter, a series of such schemes was implemented in 1985, 1997, etc., and all these schemes provided limited benefit, rather they have become an official escape route for the rich and the powerful to convert their black money into white money at a nominal cost; they confidently continue to conceal their assets, wealth and income so as to pay lower income tax rate than the normal rate.

A Word of Caution

In both the demonetization drives, many black money hoarders did not turn up to exchange their high value notes. Instead they sold them to others who could present them at the banks with less suspicion.

Raids on the premises and properties of shady individuals or companies have been performed in the past. The Income Tax department should be given more discretion to conduct raids on the premises and properties of the individuals or companies and allowed to seize the unaccounted income and wealth and take necessary legal action against the tax evaders.

Table 12: Search and Seizure Statistics 2006-12 (in crore rupees)

Financial Year	No. of Warrants	Cash	Jewelry	Other Assets	Total Assets	Total Undisclosed Income
2006-07	3534	187.48	99.19	77.96	364.64	3612.89
2007-08	3281	206.35	128.07	93.39	427.82	4160.58
2008-09	3379	339.86	122.18	88.19	550.23	4613.06
2009-10	3454	300.97	132.20	530.33	963.50	8101.35
2010-11	4852	440.28	184.15	150.55	774.98	10649.16
2011-12	5260	499.91	271.40	134.30	905.61	9289.43

Source: White Paper on Black Money, Ministry of Finance, 2012

The real estate sector is a major source of revenue for the Indian states and also a major player in the game of black money. The Real Estate (Regulation and Development) Act, 2016, makes it mandatory for builders to declare actual valuation of properties in order to prevent people from hoarding cash and doing frauds. The purpose of the act is to protect the interests of the homebuyers, bring about pan-India standardization and facilitate transparent transactions. Another major provision for protecting customer interests is that 70 percent of the amount collected from buyers for a particular project must be maintained in a separate escrow bank account and must only be used for construction of that particular project. All the Indian states are supposed to get on board within a 12-month window by creating their own rules, setting up their real estate appellate tribunals and setting up their own regulators, but the situation is a bit different in reality. A study by CRISIL (CRISIL is a global analytical company providing ratings, research, and risk and policy advisory services) shows that "Despite continuous monitoring and follow up by the Ministry of Urban Development and Housing, Government of India, only nine states (Andhra Pradesh, Bihar, Gujarat, Kerala, Madhya Pradesh, Maharashtra, Odisha, Rajasthan, and Uttar Pradesh) and six union territories (Andaman and Nicobar Islands, Chandigarh, Dadra and Nagar Haveli, Daman and Diu, Lakshadweep, and National Capital Territory of Delhi) have notified their respective Real Estate

(Regulation and Development) Rules, 2017." Though the act covers major risk areas like disclosure of the promoter and project details like project layout, land status, etc., warranties, agreements, legal recourse, penalties and standardization, yet there are certain shortcomings. Some of the shortcomings are a lengthy approval process may delay project launch, and such delays may in turn lead to fewer buying options for homebuyers. But the advantages of this act aim to weed out unfair players from the sector in a phased manner in order to make this sector a more organized one.

Apart from demonetization drives and voluntary disclosure schemes, special bearer bonds, income tax raids, amnesty schemes, Indira Vikas Patra, NRI foreign exchange remittance, etc., were some of the other measures used to curb the menace of black money in the past. However, all these measures taken to tackle the problem have not given cent percent results. Special bearer bonds are bonds whose owner's name is not on record with the bond's issuer. Under such schemes, any person holding black money can buy such bonds. The person purchasing such bonds will not be questioned about her/his identity and the source of her/his income. The special bearer bonds scheme (1981) was a major one launched by the Indian Government as an income disclosure scheme. Under this scheme anyone could buy these bonds, even with anonymity, and would not be scrutinized or investigated by the tax authorities, and premium on redemption of these bonds was also exempted from tax. These bonds could be bought with foreign currency also. All the provisions and norms related to these bonds are stated in the Special Bearer Bonds (Immunities and Exemptions) Act, 1981. Another famous bearer bond scheme, issued in the year 1986 through post offices, was the Indira Vikas Patra. The Indian Government has launched several such amnesty schemes from time to time (Voluntary Disclosure Scheme, 1951 and 1965, National Defense Gold Bonds, National Housing Bank Deposit Scheme, 1991, etc.) whereby tax defaulters are allowed to pay a tax, waiving or minimizing the interests and penalties. Also the defaulters would not be asked any further questions and would be allowed to convert their income and wealth into legitimate money, which facilitates the Indian Government to collect taxes and pump back legitimate money into the Indian economy. In the largest-ever declaration of black money, 65,250 crore rupees was declared as unaccounted income and assets under the government's Income Declaration Scheme (IDS) 2016. Such voluntary disclosure has been adopted by the Indian Government in the past and it can be launched in the future too. The following table gives data on the amount of undisclosed income detected during the period 2006-12.

Table 13: Amount of Undisclosed Income Detected During the Period 2006-12

Financial Year	No. of Surveys Conducted	Undisclosed Income Detected (in crore)
2006-07	6,207	2,612.77
2007-08	6,071	3,581.77
2008-09	5,777	3,059.89
2009-10	4,680	4,857.10
2010-11	3,911	5,894.44
2011-12	3,706	6,572.75

Source: Whitepaper on Black Money

6.2 INSTITUTIONS, AGENCIES, MEASURES AND REFORMS

There are a number of Indian institutions (Income Tax Department, Central Board of Direct Taxes, Central Board of Excise and Customs, Central Bureau of Investigation, etc.) that do all they can do to curb the menace of black money. Tax evaders operate across borders whereas tax administration is limited to national borders. This transnational nature of transferring money to other nations in order to avoid evasion or conceal assets needs combined efforts of all nations of the world in terms of bilateral and multilateral cooperation. These transnational efforts have been discussed throughout the book and for these efforts to succeed, each nation needs a solid local tax regime and empowered authorities and agencies to work hand-in-hand with their global counterparts. The first institution of India in this fight against black money that comes to mind is the Income Tax (IT) department and then the rest follow.

1. Income Tax (IT) Department—this department has created a special e-mail address where anyone can provide tip-off information regarding tax evasion and money laundering.

After the demonetization drive of 2016, the Income Tax department launched Operation Clean Money. The first phase of the operation involved e-verification of large cash deposits made during 9 November to 30 December 2016. The second phase included risk classification, wherein this department had identified high risk cases of one lakh people.

This department detected undisclosed income of 13,715 crore rupees through 12,526 surveys in the period 2016-17.

2. Central Board of Direct Taxes (CBDT)—this department is a division of the Ministry of Finance under the Department of Revenue and is responsible for the administration of direct tax laws through the Income Tax Department. It also provides critical inputs for policy-making and planning of levy and collection of direct taxes. It also proposes changes in direct tax enactments, structure and rates as per the policies of the Indian government.

To discharge its functions properly, CBDT is aided by various directorates that are specialized in various areas like inspection, recovery, training, etc. The CBDT has come out with a draft notification seeking stakeholders' comment on filing of Form 28AA by giving details of income and advance taxes paid. Businesses have to specify reason for any reduction in advance tax payment compared to preceding financial year. This information will help to give an idea about the trend of income of the assessee on an almost real time basis.

3. Central Board of Excise and Customs (CBEC)—is a part of the Department of Revenue. It has been renamed and reorganized as the Central Board of Indirect Taxes and Customs (CIBC) as a part of the GST rollout. It is an integral wing of the Indian Government in its fight against black money; it has been strengthened and expanded to effectively fight against black money. This department comes under the Department of Revenue, Ministry of Finance. The main reason for the name change is due to the overhauling of the tax structure in India with the introduction of the indirect tax reform, Goods and Services Tax.

CIBC has also assisted the Indian Government in policy making in relation to GST. At the same time, this department will continue to perform the earlier central excise levy and customs functions. CIBC has undergone rigorous restructuring in order to ensure proper rendering of taxpayer services to all the taxpayers through an indirect tax administration structure having an all-India presence.

4. Central Bureau of Investigation (CBI)—it is the premier investigative agency in India. Its main aims are to improve transparency in government, to handle criminal cases related to frauds and corruption committed by public servants, special crimes like terrorism, mafia-related crimes and economic crimes like financial frauds, smuggling, etc. CBI has also opined that the Mutual Legal Assistance Treaty (MLAT) needs to be signed with many more nations. MLAT is an agreement between two or more nations that allows exchange of information and evidence related to criminal and related cases, including black money and money laundering cases.

In the year 2015, a total of 673 corruption cases were registered by the CBI involving 1,300+ public servants. In the post-demonetization period, the government's focus is on greater collaboration between the tax department and other investigating agencies, inducing CBI, to ensure that those caught with substantial amounts of unaccounted money are simultaneously probed for corruption and black money. In the period from 2014 to 2017, through its probe into various loan fraud cases, CBI unearthed a complex web of 339 shell companies used for allegedly diverting funds to the tune of 2,900 crore rupees.

5. Central Vigilance Commission (CVC)—CVC has always shown strong support for improved governance to keep a tab on black money. It has always expressed the following *mantra* on several occasions: "Accountability along with addressing bureaucratic delays and effective public grievance redressal mechanism is the way forward." It also believes in the participation of the civil society, whereby the various participants of the civil society can report information against public servants who are in possession of black money or assets.

CVC has been assigned with the task of enforcing the Prevention of Corruption Act so far as public servants of Indian Government are concerned. CBI's investigation work relating to corruption cases is also monitored by CVC. CVC has also been included in the list of government agencies authorized to seek details from Financial Intelligence Unit (FIU) on doubtful banking transactions of government employees. The main aim of this arrangement is to block all channels of routing black money through the banking system.

6. The Indian Government completed the process of ratification of the **United Nations Convention Against Corruption (UNCAC)** in 2011, six years after signing this convention. UNCAC is the first globally legally binding international anti-corruption instrument; it a landmark convention not only in terms of its wide coverage but also for its provisions and practices like tracing, freezing and confiscating the proceeds of corruption, sharing good practices, comprehensive set of standards, rules and measures for strengthening legal and regulatory regimes to fight corruption, research, peer reviews, training, etc. This transnational move is an important milestone in India's role in the global economy and in combating the supply side of the corruption equation in order to minimize the loss of current and future business. This move will help India to seize unlawful money and assets and to deal with the problem of black money and corruption through administrative reforms and legislative measures. This convention requires criminalizing the act of foreign bribery; hence the Indian Government has drafted the Prevention of Bribery of Foreign Public Officials and Officials of Public International Organizations Bill 2011. This Bill empowers the Indian Government to enter into agreements with other nations for enforcing this law and for exchanging investigative information. It criminalizes the acceptance or solicitation of bribes by both foreign public officials and officials of public international organizations for obtaining or retaining business

as well as abetting or attempting the above acts (*Corruption in India: Causes, Effects and Reforms*, Chitra G. Lele, 2015).

7. **Tax Information Exchange Agreements** (TIEA)—to further the cause of tax cooperation and to curb the menace of black money, India has signed TIEA with several nations like the British Virgin Islands, the Bahamas, Bermuda, etc. Such agreements call for transparent sharing of financial information in terms of ownership details, banking details, etc., and other features include tax examination in territory of another party, criminal or civil tax investigation matters, etc. India has always been a strong supporter of international cooperation with respect to exchange of information.

The Special Investigation Team (SIT) concluded that the lack of legal frameworks and treaties between India and tax havens is one of the main obstacles in bringing back illicit money stashed away in these havens. After submitting its report to the Indian Government, based on this observation of SIT, the government has taken steps in signing several such treaties.

The scope of these treaties needs to be expanded in order for India and other nations to curb illicit financial flows. Currently, they are mainly focused on data and information collection with additional measures; the scope needs to include actual seizure of or attachment on money and assets of potential Indian black money holders in order to facilitate quick legal action. Moreover, until all tax havens sign such treaties with all countries, illicit financial flows will continue to find other channels.

8. **Directorate of Criminal Investigation**—it is an intelligence gathering, analysis and dissemination wing of the Income Tax department. It studies and analysis data from various agencies like Enforcement Directorate, Financial Intelligence Unit, etc., and reports its findings to the Income Tax department and its probe units, based on which raids and seizures of money and assets are carried out to curb black money and tax evasion.

This wing is also entrusted with the responsibility of studying and preparing trends of economic crimes, which would include detection and analysis of any terror funds in the economic channels.

9. Financial Intelligence Unit (FIU)—FIU is an independent body reporting directly to the Economic Intelligence Council (EIC is the apex forum responsible for the coordination among various government agencies that deal with economic offences). FIU's main aim is to provide timely financial intelligence and information for safeguarding the interests of all the players of the financial systems and intermediaries from black money channels, hawala transactions, terrorism funding, money laundering and several other financial crimes.

FIU has an arrangement of sharing intelligence and information with the CVC, CBI, RBI, National Investigation Agency (NIA has been established to combat terror in India), Intelligence Bureau (IB is India's internal intelligence agency), Supreme Court-appointed Special Investigation Team, and several other agencies to deal with cases of collusion between private persons/organizations and government employees involving black money and several other financial crimes.

For all investigation and intelligence institutions to work efficiently, the data mining and analysis capabilities need to be strengthened with proper risk analysis tools. With so much of information and files to be studied, a computerized system and technical infrastructure are a must. The transition from paper records to computer files is a must to keep up with the changing nature of financial flows and global trade, and also to facilitate quicker automatic exchange of information.

Just like the US has a capable intelligence system of gathering information called the Internal Revenue Service (IRS is the revenue service of the United States Federal Government), India needs to set up such agencies to address the basic and structural flaws in the entire information and intelligence gathering processes. The policing of society and its nefarious elements have always been a product of various crises and scandals. The current Indian intelligence and investigation agencies need to incorporate and adapt the good practices from the US IRS and then apply these good practices to meaningful and timely intelligence to fight against black money.

The intelligence and investigation agencies in India are always under the clout of their political bosses. Their work is often influenced by selfish political agendas, which puts a roadblock in their investigating processes. Hence, a strong and impartial legal and administrative framework for these agencies is a must, where they are answerable to only third-party impartial people. Such a framework needs to ensure that these agencies will be given the required legal infrastructure and support to uphold the law, and they will not have to compromise any of their duties for political agendas.

Another important factor that needs to be incorporated is Know Your Customer (KYC) and this is an important measure in curbing money laundering. Financial institutions need to initiate the KYC process and norms and ask for Permanent Account Number (PAN) on a compulsory basis for all financial transactions. Besides this, all financial institutions need to verify the source of income and funds, keep track of all irregular transactions and monitor all the activities done through the accounts.

Yet another important aspect that needs to be taken care of for all these institutions to work effectively is personnel training so as to upgrade skills and level of awareness. Especially in the case of exchange of information, employees need to be trained and made fully aware of the dynamics and provisions of the various treaties and their latest updates and developments. Employees also need to be trained in framing appropriate information requests so that the treaty countries understand the exact requirement and produce the required information in a timely manner. The Global Forum, along with a select group of developed nations, is willing to aid developing countries in the process of building capacity. India too is willing to set up a regional centre which would act as mentor for SAARC nations. For bringing about transparency and accountability in all sectors and at all levels, it is of utmost importance to set up robust vigilance and oversight mechanisms and best practices.

6.3 PUBLIC PULSE, PROTESTS AND OPINIONS

The word on the street is often close to the truth. It is high time that the citizenry becomes vigilant and active. It needs to raise its collective voice to register its protest against the menace of black money. "Corruption along with Black money" has been at the top of the agenda of widespread public protests. It is time for the Indian Government to adopt the upgraded meaning of governance, which now means to facilitate and not to dominate the public. The public pulse should be taken into account by the Indian Government while framing policies and measures, including the ones against black money. The Indian Government needs to understand the role of civil society in order to gain a better understanding of their opinions and suggestions against black money, which are expressed through various ways like protests and rallies. The civil society includes community-based organizations, social activists, community leaders, non-governmental organizations, human rights organizations, research organizations, pressure groups, etc.

Moral education in terms of instilling values of honesty and integrity should begin within the four walls of each and every home in India. Only then we can act as vigilant citizens and prevent fair setups from degenerating into pits of black money. Apart from such education, seminars and workshops should be held for the masses in order to educate them about the latest happenings about black money and its dynamics.

Civic oversight monitoring of public institutions, government policies and practices, and provincial administration through citizens' initiatives, public forums and community leaders is highly needed in India.

A Word of Caution

The masses need to be careful of their dormant accounts as they can be easily used for conducting money laundering activities. One should not share one's bank account number with strangers, especially with people who ask to help them transfer money from foreign places to India, and they may offer a commission for using the bank accounts, but one needs to completely decline such offers or else one can inadvertently become a part of such money laundering activities.

Section 10(1) of the Income Tax Act, 1961, exempts agricultural income from taxation by the Central Government. As per the latest National Sample Survey data, the landholding pattern of agricultural households shows that the vast majority, almost 70 percent have marginal holdings of below one hectare, and a very small percentage, only 0.4 percent hold significant lands of over 10 hectares. By even taxing the income of this small yet top portion the agriculture community, a large sum can be collected as agriculture income tax. There is scope of imposing tax not only on rich individual farmers, but also on large multinational companies in the field of agriculture. This sector has been a tax shelter for a long time. Tax evaders use this sector to convert their black money into white by showing ownership of ancestral property in villages and showing that they are using this property for agricultural produce by providing fabricated receipts related to agricultural activities. Agriculture income should be taxed for those who are earning money both through agricultural as well as non-agricultural sources. Rich farmers and multinational companies must be taxed in order to protect the interests of small and marginal farmers.

Media professional should also play an integral role in this anti-black money drive. Independent journalism should play an active role in exposing black money and all corruption-related scams. Media professionals and journalists should be trained and equipped with the tools of analysis to investigate scams. Freedom of information should be strengthened so that a free media can perform its role as a vigilant watchdog without fear of reprisal or harassment from the higher-ups.

Public opinions and polls related to black money need to be conducted on a regular basis and the inputs collected and collated from these need to be taken into consideration while framing new laws or re-looking at and making changes in the existing laws. Public pressure is necessary for bringing about a better recovery of black money and expose of the names involved in it.

Professional bodies that keep a watch on banking institutions, company secretaries, solicitors and lawyers, chartered accountants, etc., should increase the frequency of monitoring mechanisms and carry out independent inspections of dealings and transactions related to hawala and money laundering.

The details of aberrant taxpayers who have been caught for evasion or concealment of income, assets, wealth, etc., should be published in the gazette as well as in the press. All the details in terms of their names, amount of evasion, penalties, etc., should be shared with the public. If the assessee is a company, the names of all the board members, directors or partners should be made public.

> **Spotlight**
>
> The agenda for action needs to include various reforms, aspects and mechanisms like tools for engaging citizens, strengthening of RTI as an instrument for enhancing government transparency, strengthening of political will and political culture, participatory performance monitoring, focus groups for supporting the citizen voice, etc.

The rise of people power is needed—connecting the agents of change. Unless and until we do not act as responsible citizens and become willing to change our attitudes and live by the morals of truth and integrity, we won't be able to reconstruct a black money-free society with an enhanced level of public accountability. It is all about minimizing conflicts of interests and maximizing the common good through reforms in all fields and at all levels.

6.4 ACTS, BILLS, LAWS, POLICIES, PROPOSALS AND TREATIES

In recent times, the Indian Government had passed the Undisclosed Foreign Income and Assets (Imposition of Tax) Bill, 2015, with an aim of unearthing black money stashed abroad. The main features of this Bill are: it empowers the government to enter into agreements with other nations for the exchange of information related to tax evasion and black money, it also states an exchange punishment clause of jail for 3 to 10 years for tax evasions on foreign income along with a penalty equal to three times the amount of tax evaded or 90 percent of the undisclosed income or the value of the asset, it also states that tax on all foreign income will have to be paid at the flat rate of 30 percent without deduction, exemption, set off or carry forward losses that the Income Tax Act permits, and finally there will be a limited compliance time window. This act gives an opportunity to the black money holders to voluntarily disclose their black money and undeclared assets abroad, and pay a tax within a compliance window time to regularize the same or else the black money holders will have to face severe penal and prosecution measures. There were 648 declarations involving undisclosed foreign assets worth ₹ 4,164 crore rupees made when the Indian Government gave a one-time three months compliance window.

There are very broad legislations and laws in India against the practices of money laundering which includes all crimes and offences except offences related to drug trafficking or offences under Indian Penal Code. As far as drug offences are concerned, prevention of money laundering is taken care of by the Narcotic and Psychotropic Substances Act, 1985. The Prevention of Money Laundering Act (PMLA), 2002, provides provisions for punishment in money laundering and black money hoarding cases. It provides for the seizure and confiscation of property and other assets derived from money laundering. This act was enacted in 2002, but was amended thrice, first in 2005, then in 2009 and then in 2012. The 2012 amendment has enlarged the definition of money laundering. The Reserve Bank of India, the Insurance Regulatory and Development Authority and the Securities and Exchange Board of India adhere to the rules and provisions of this act; hence this act and its provisions are applicable to all financial institutions, banks, insurance companies and mutual funds. The Directorate of Enforcement in the Department of Revenue is entrusted with the responsibility of investigating the cases of money laundering under the Prevention of Money Laundering Act, 2002. One of the major amendments of this act includes the provision to confiscate domestically held property which is equal in value to the property held abroad.

In recent times, in 2014, India had also set up a Special Investigation Team (SIT) consisting of a panel of the heads of a number of the nation's high-profile enforcement, financial probe and investigating agencies. The SIT was appointed by the Indian Government on the directions of the Supreme Court. The SIT was constituted to oversee the investigation process into cases involving allegations of unaccounted or black money: cases where investigation is completed, waiting to be initiated or investigation has already started. RBI on June 23, 2014, ordered all the banks and financial institutions to provide information sought by the SIT in this regards. The SIT has also been instructed to file periodic reports to the Supreme Court informing it of the status of their work from time to time. According to the SIT, for tracking and curbing illicit financial flows out of the nation, use of the Reserve Bank of India data by various government departments and law enforcement agencies like Directorate of Revenue Intelligence, Enforcement Directorate, etc., is a must. The SIT also strongly suggested to the Indian Government that there needs to be renegotiation of the Double Taxation Avoidance Agreements (DTAAs) with countries in order to get accurate information about the various cases that need to be tackled; detailed information is needed in order to tackle cases related to the money maintained by Indians in foreign nations. Diplomatic level talks are needed with other nations to get these treaties amended to help bring back the black money to India. The SIT also suggested stronger regulatory laws and penalties, and also to introduce legislative reforms in existing laws like the Prevention of Money Laundering Act.

Rationalization of regulatory reforms and tax structure is necessary for curbing the black money inflows into and outflows from India. A simple and transparent tax system will encourage citizens at all levels to try to at least comply with the tax laws. A rational and reasonable level of incentive for compliance is needed to be incorporated in the tax regime.

Several experts have proposed a number of ways to the Indian Government for bringing back black money stashed away in foreign banks in countries such as Switzerland, Mauritius, the Virgin Islands, etc. For instance, K.V.M. Pai, the former chief commissioner of income tax, had proposed an amnesty that offers immunity with conditions such as a tax of 30 percent plus interest. He had also proposed for the incorporation of a clause in the income tax return, requiring taxpayers to provide details of their foreign accounts. Further, he had also recommended administrative measures to gather intelligence on those who do not disclose their foreign accounts.

Mauritius accounts for over 40 percent of FDI flows into India and in the wake of scams like 2G Spectrum and IPL where the money trail led to this tax haven, the tax structure needs to be reformed in such a way that the income tax return declaration makes it mandatory for taxpayers to give details of their foreign accounts. To curb black money, India and its government will have to find ways of attracting FDI into India through fair channels.

Combined reporting should be implemented for multinational corporations. It is the practice of treating the parent and subsidiary companies of a multinational corporation as one business entity for the purpose of tax calculations. Adding up all the profits earned worldwide by a corporation, and then taxing a share of these combined total profits according to the level of activity in each nation would help in minimizing the tax benefits of shifting incomes and profits to tax havens.

A strict policy of transparency should be implemented in regards to political parties and their functioning and electoral funding. Politicians and their parties themselves should agree to be included within the ambit of the Right to Information Act. A strong political will by all political leaders is needed to cooperate with the government, Law Commission and Election Commission. All these stakeholders need to work in unison to study all the angles related to electoral funding and come up with measures and recommendations that are needed to bring about transparency in the operations of political parties.

Due to the pressure put on Switzerland by India and other nations, Switzerland has agreed to provide information and assistance to foreign countries in their pursuit of black money. A similar approach should be adopted across the globe to curb both local and global black money flows.

Globalization and relaxation of foreign controls has led to an increase in cross-border transactions. These international business opportunities give tax evaders greater opportunities for tax evasion and hoarding black money as compared to tax evaders who operate only in domestic markets. Therefore, it is important for various domestic and global tax authorities and administrators to cooperate with each other to nab the wrongdoers. One of the major ways of achieving this international cooperation is through exchange of key information through instruments of exchanging information like Tax Information Exchange Agreement (TIEA) and Double Tax Avoidance Agreement (DTAA). TIEA allows for tax examination abroad and has specific provisions for providing banking and ownership information. The main aim of TIEA is to promote international cooperation in tax matters through exchange of information. DTAA is a treaty to ensure that the same income is not taxed twice; it is an economic agreement between two or more countries that aims to avoid double taxation of the same income in two or more countries. DTAA can either be comprehensive to cover all sources of income or be limited to certain sources such as taxing of income from transport, shipping, etc. DTAAs are necessary for the growth of the Indian economy as they provide clarity on how certain cross-border transactions will be taxed and this encourages foreign investors to enter the Indian markets. In the last 2+ years, India has completed negotiation of 62 DTAAs/TIEAs and has signed 33 DTAAs/TIEAs. There is always a lot of talk about information exchange, but no one is ready to walk the talk.

The Multilateral Convention on Mutual Administrative Assistance in Tax Matters (MCMAA) is an OECD multilateral tax convention used to promote international cooperation in matters related to taxes like tax collection, tax examination, automatic information exchange, information exchange on request, etc. It is the most comprehensive convention available for all forms of tax cooperation to deal with tax evasion and avoidance. This instrument is multilateral as against the DTAAs/TIEAs which are mostly bilateral in nature. The MCMAA provides all types of administrative assistance and cooperation between nations. India has ratified the MCMAA in 2012. This move has helped to reinforce and strengthen the partnership of OECD and India in matters related to taxes.

India has actively participated and contributed inputs to the development process of the ongoing multilateral OECD Base Erosion and Profit Shifting initiative. The Indian Government in its response to the UN questionnaire regarding its experience related to BEPS had identified the following as the common practices of BEPS in India: treaty shopping (treaty shopping is the practice of structuring a multinational business in such a way so as to take advantage of more favorable tax treaties, especially available in certain jurisdictions or nations), non-taxation of digital economy in country of source, and shifting of profits by aggressive transfer pricing by way of payments to foreign affiliated companies. A number of proposals and recommendations in the Indian Finance Act, 2016, are influenced by the recommendations in this initiative. India has signed this multilateral initiative to be able to fill the loopholes in various tax treaties worldwide so as to resolve treaty disputes. This move by the Indian Government will help it to minimize inconsistencies among global tax treaties and regimes.

Income Tax Overseas Units (ITOUs) are needed to facilitate cooperation in various areas like information exchange, taxation of cross-border transactions, assistance in collection of taxes, etc. India has set up several such ITOUs in nations like France, Japan, USA, etc., and should continue to set up such ITOUs in order to facilitate coordination with the competent authority offices of the foreign countries on real-time basis so as to deal with matters related to black money.

The Fiscal Responsibility and Budget Management Act, 2003, is a fiscal sector act to institutionalize fiscal discipline and fiscal consolidation. Its aim is to achieve better coordination between fiscal and monetary policy, reduce revenue deficits and fiscal deficits, and bring about transparency in the fiscal operations of the Indian Government.

India is associated with organizations like the Bay of Bengal Initiative for Multi-Sectoral Technical and Economic

Cooperation (BIMSTEC). BIMSTEC is a sub-regional organization comprising of seven nations of South Asia and South East Asia (Bangladesh, Nepal, Bhutan, India, Sri Lanka Myanmar and Thailand) that collaborate on issues related to terrorism, black money and transnational crimes.

In order to ensure a fair allocation of natural and man-made resources, especially scarce resources like minerals, telecom, etc., a proper grievance redressal system and oversight in the form of regulations needs to be implemented immediately.

Faulty practices like round tripping, hawala transactions, shell companies, excessive banking secrecy and complex global laws need to be replaced with people-oriented leadership, vigilant civil society, good governance at all levels and strict policy implementation. There needs to be higher penalties, tougher punishments and longer jail terms for all the miscreants who hide undeclared cash and assets outside their own nations. Also the supporting elements of shell companies, foreign banks, etc., need to be brought under this scope of punishments and penalties.

The Indian Government can also deliberate providing tax incentives for use of credit and debit cards as practiced in countries such as Korea. But again such deliberations need to be implemented carefully in order to maximize their effectiveness.

Spotlight

For all the current and future acts, bills, laws, policies, proposals and treaties to function properly, both the Central and State governments need to work in unison. For this to happen, the power struggles between the two levels needs to be minimized. This decentralization of all measures is necessary so that the full benefits reach the public, and do not get diluted.

6.5 FEW FINAL THOUGHTS

We all know that complete eradication of black money is impossible, it can only be minimized. All the estimates, data and statistics shared in this book are just the tip of the iceberg. Black money is a huge market for people with legitimate cash and those with illegitimate cash as well. All are trying to maximize their profits while dodging taxes. The obsession for money, especially black money, has been the driving factor for the downfall of mankind. Black money is like a big black hole in the Indian economy. The indirect costs of black money like degradation of moral fiber, unemployment, economic distortions, etc., are far more than the direct cost of revenue losses.

For the last several decades, "bringing black money back" has remained a favorite slogan of several political parties to woo their voters. But all in vain! In the last few years, India has witnessed a spate of laws and regulations, but by merely introducing new laws and regulations does not really target the top segment of the economy. Instead of the top segment facing the brunt, the real victims of additional laws and regulations are the honest and hardworking taxpayers.

Through drives, schemes and laws, some unaccounted money and wealth can be recovered or seized, but people will eventually find more and more ingenious ways to convert their unaccounted money and wealth into white money. Reducing black money without putting an end to its sources is no strategy at all. A strong political will along with a multi-pronged strategy is needed wherein first the growth of the parallel economy needs to be thwarted, then the conversion of black into white money needs to be stopped, and along with this, all sectors that help in generating and parking black money need to be brought under the scanner of the authorities.

The practice of abrupt transfers of sincere officers of the government investigation agencies should be stopped immediately because only such sincere government officers can bring all black money offenders to book. Only they can encourage whistle blowers to come forward with hard-hitting facts and evidence that can make the public aware of all the high-profile black money cases. Each time a high-profile case is reported and sincere officers begin their work of unearthing all the details, there are sudden transfers and terminations, and these cases and criminals are never punished. Bureaucratic and political pressure needs to be completely eliminated so that sincere investigating officers can fulfill their duties in all sincerity.

Training all types of professionals who deal with curbing black money is a must. Imparting appropriate skills of investigation and evidence collection to personnel is needed to bring about effective actions against black money hoarders. Governments in several countries, including India, need to implement bilateral and multilateral mechanisms in several areas, including training, in order to deal with the various evils of black money.

The instruments of a clean economy have to be smarter than they have been in the past. Legal loopholes and loose ends need to be corrected in order to prevent the generation of black money through money laundering, hawala transfer of money and assets, electoral funding and tax havens. Political funding and corporate lobbying should be brought within the ambit of Right to Information Act. There are several inactive political parties that are used for parking black money. Such inactive parties need to be deregistered by the Election Commission of India. In the Union Budget of 2017, a proposal was made that stated political parties have to file their income tax returns within a given time limit but no strict penal provision has been put in place.

The Ministry of Rural Development has set an ambitious target to have 35 million job accounts linked to Aadhaar-linked bank accounts to enable the digital drive initiative of the Indian Government. Several such steps are underway to facilitate the digital economy culture in India. But mere linking or enrollment of people in such digitization schemes is not enough as the opportunities for actual digital transactions are limited in India. Both training and opportunities are needed for introducing the culture of digitization in India. Another aspect of introducing the digital economy is data security and cyber crimes. India needs to work in a vigilant manner in all these matters.

The 2016 policy of demonetization may be viewed as a step in the direction of curbing the black money menace. But mere demonetization is not sufficient. The earlier demonetization drives, instead of causing a dent in the black money economy, rather caused an increase in black money resources and a similar scenario has been seen with the 2016 demonetization policy. Such policies can become effective only when they have the support of strict regulations and structural reforms. Also this problem needs to be solved at the source, or as usual black money will strike back. The Indian Government must implement provisions that will reduce the opportunities and incentives for generating black money by narrowing the gap between the market value and the one fixed by the India Government agencies for different duties. Apart from curbing the generation aspect, the Indian Government also needs to tackle the conversion component. The Indian Government should prioritize taxing the super-rich and not the common man.

According to the Economic and Social Survey of Asia and the Pacific of 2017, "The measure (demonetization of 2016) did not, by itself, impede future black money flows in new denominations. Broader structural reforms which could also contribute to enhanced transparency include: the implementation of a goods and services tax; voluntary disclosure of income scheme; and tracking of high-value transactions through taxpayer identification numbers."

> **Spotlight**
>
> India needs to quickly adopt a holistic approach to implement appropriate reforms within its boundaries, and to collaborate with other nations in its fight against the menace of black money.

Collective complacency needs to be replaced with collective consciousness of responsibility, transparency and accountability. People will always find newer ways to make and conceal black money, and this tendency and attitude will continue to gnaw at the foundation of the society and erode the base of moral values. It is high time that the unethical practices of generating black money need to be tackled head on. Collective action is needed or else black money will continue to propagate dishonesty and shatter the faith of the common man in the moral values of honesty, hard work and sincerity.

Awareness and financial literacy in the population, both educated middle class and illiterate rural class, regarding how reporting of taxes and subsequent generation of revenue from it will ultimately help in nation building is a must. Massive sensitization campaigns should be conducted in order to raise the level of awareness about the destructive impact of black money and its dynamics. We as a collective consciousness need to study the multiple perspectives and the ever-changing dynamics of black money and its players, and then propose a multi-pronged agenda of reform that has the potential to minimize black money, to a considerable extent.

This is a good time to start!

6.6 CHAPTER RECAP

1. India and all its stakeholders need to adopt a multi-pronged, well-coordinated approach. Apart from rationalization of tax rates, what is also needed to make this approach more effective, is effective implementation of tax laws and necessary changes in public perception about tax evasion and black money.

2. The main weakness of all anti-black money programs and methods is that they touch the problem of black money already created but they do not go into the root cause of the generation of black money. The key element of tackling this huge problem of black money includes prevention of generation of black money, effective detection of black money, foolproof investigation and immediate justice.

3. Apart from demonetization drives and voluntary disclosure schemes, special bearer bonds, income tax raids, amnesty schemes, Indira Vikas Patra, NRI foreign exchange remittance, etc., were some of the other measures used to curb the menace of black money in the past.

4. There are a number of Indian institutions (Income Tax Department, Central Board of Direct Taxes, Central Board of Excise and Customs, Central Bureau of Investigation, etc.) that do all they can do to curb the menace of black money. Tax evaders operate across borders whereas tax administration is limited to national borders. This trans-national nature of transferring money to other nations in order to avoid evasion or conceal assets needs combined efforts of all nations of the world in terms of bilateral and multilateral cooperation.

5. The intelligence and investigation agencies in India are always under the clout of their political bosses. Their work is often influenced by selfish political agendas, which puts a roadblock in their investigating processes. Hence, a strong and impartial legal and administrative framework for these agencies is a must, where they are answerable to only third-party impartial people.

6. The word on the street is often close to the truth. It is high time that the citizenry becomes vigilant and active. It needs to raise its collective voice to register its protest against the menace of black money.

7. Moral education in terms of instilling values of honesty and integrity should begin within the four walls of each and every home in India. Only then we can act as vigilant citizens and prevent fair setups from degenerating into pits of black money. Apart from such education, seminars and workshops should be held for the masses in order to educate them about the latest happenings about black money and its dynamics.

8. Civic oversight monitoring of public institutions, government policies and practices, and provincial administration through citizens' initiatives, public forums and community leaders is highly needed in India.

9. Agriculture income should be taxed for those who are earning money both through agricultural as well as non-agricultural sources. Rich farmers and multinational companies must be taxed in order to protect the interests of small and marginal farmers.

10. In recent times, the Indian Government had passed the Undisclosed Foreign Income and Assets (Imposition of Tax) Bill, 2015, with an aim of unearthing black money stashed abroad.

11. Globalization and relaxation of foreign controls has led to an increase in cross-border transactions. These international business opportunities give tax evaders greater opportunities for tax evasion and hoarding black money as compared to tax evaders who operate only in domestic markets. Therefore, it is important for various domestic and global tax authorities and administrators to cooperate with each other to nab the wrongdoers. One of the major ways of achieving this international cooperation is through exchange of key information through instruments of exchanging information like Tax Information Exchange Agreement (TIEA) and Double Tax Avoidance Agreement (DTAA).

12. Faulty practices like round tripping, hawala transactions, shell companies, excessive banking secrecy and complex global laws need to be replaced with people-oriented leadership, vigilant civil society, good governance at all levels and strict policy implementation.

13. The obsession for money, especially black money, has been the driving factor for the downfall of mankind. Black money is like a big black hole in the Indian economy. The indirect costs of black money like degradation of moral fiber, unemployment, economic distortions, etc., are far more than the direct cost of revenue losses.

14. The instruments of a clean economy have to be smarter than they have been in the past. Legal loopholes and loose ends need to be corrected in order to prevent the generation of black money through money laundering, hawala transfer of money and assets, electoral funding and tax havens.

15. The practice of abrupt transfers of sincere officers of the government investigation agencies should be stopped immediately because only such sincere government officers can bring all black money offenders to book.

16. Massive sensitization campaigns should be conducted in order to raise the level of awareness about the destructive impact of black money and its dynamics.

6.7 QUESTIONS FOR REFLECTION

1. What is the main weakness of all anti-black money programs and methods?
2. What measures can be taken to enhance the effectives of various anti-black money acts, bills, laws, policies, proposals and treaties?
3. What is the role of technology in the facilitation of apprehending tax evaders?

4. How can faulty practices related to black money be eliminated?
5. What is the role of civil society in the fight against black money?
6. How can the various governmental institutions be improved to curb the menace of black money and tax evasion?
7. How can the various domestic and global tax authorities and administrators cooperate with each other to nab the wrongdoers?

Author Information

Chitra Lele is a young award-winning poet, world record holder, research scholar, record-setting author and software consultant. She is a double postgraduate: Master in Computer Management and Master of Science in Software Engineering. She holds several professional certifications in the field of software project management (CompTIA Project+Certification in Project Management, Microsoft Certified Technology Specialist and many more). She has an excellent academic record. Her publications include scholarly articles and research papers, poetry anthologies, novels, and academic and reference books. She is the associate editor of the *Eternity* journal.

Chitra has been conferred with the title of "A Versatile Writer" by the India Book of Records. She set this record by penning maximum number of books in a short span of 18 months. The books belong to various genres, right from poetry to business management and from personal transformation to social studies. Her books have set a string of world records, received positive reviews, and garnered praise from world leaders, award-winning poets, best-selling authors, management gurus and business experts. Some of Chitra's titles are *Corruption in India: Causes, Effects and Reforms, Divine Decorations, Organizational Democracy, Call Center Essentials: A Practical Guide to Real-Time Results, English Language: The Gateway to Global Growth, The 6 Spheres of Life: Unlocking the Door to*

Success and Happiness, *Waltz to the Future: A Divine Dance of Perfumed Poems*, and many more. Her books certainly will be a valuable addition to your home as well as office library, and will help you to reach your goals and conquer new frontiers.

For more information about Chitra's professional management career, academic and reference books, literary awards, media mentions, poetry books, world records and much more, please visit her creative and academic blog: http://chitrathesavvysynergist.blogspot.in/p/about-me_20.html

B/219